ANGELA GALLOP

How to Solve a Crime

Real Cases from the Cutting Edge of Forensics

With Jane Smith

HODDER &
STOUGHTON

First published in Great Britain in 2022 by Hodder & Stoughton
An Hachette UK company

1

Copyright © Angela Gallop and Jane Smith 2022

A CIP catalogue record for this title is available from the British Library

Hardback ISBN 9781529331349
Trade Paperback ISBN 9781529331356

Typeset in Plantin Light by Hewer Text UK Ltd, Edinburgh
Printed and bound in Great Britain by Clays Ltd, Elcograf S.p.A.

Hodder & Stoughton policy is to use papers that are natural, renewable
and recyclable products and made from wood grown in sustainable
forests. The logging and manufacturing processes are expected to
conform to the environmental regulations of the country of origin.

Hodder & Stoughton Ltd
Carmelite House
50 Victoria Embankment
London EC4Y 0DZ

www.hodder.co.uk

To the many scientists and other professionals I've worked with – originally in the Forensic Science Service, and then in Forensic Access, Forensic Alliance/LGC Forensics, and latterly Axiom International – and who have taught me so many interesting things and elevated my own endeavours to whole new levels. I am immensely grateful to you all.

Acknowledgements

I would like to acknowledge all of the people who have contributed to this book in one way or another, all whom I have admired and many of whom I have personally worked with over the years. They include in particular:

Dr Samantha Pickles
Dr Alex Allan
Professor Sue Black
Dr Marjorie Turner
Ed Jarman
Dr Itiel Dror
Peter Swann
Dr Clive Candy
Dr Mike Jenkins
Nigel Kelly
April Robson
Dr Philip Avenell
Deb Hopwood
Dr Ian Evett
Caroline Crawford
Dr Richard Shepherd
David Martin

The Links Group
Dr Anthony Peabody
Huw Griffiths
Geoff Arnold
Roy Green
Stephen Cole
Damian Walton
Dr Chris Davies
Professor Peter French
Russell Stockdale
Denise Stanworth
Professor Robert Forrest
Professor Roger Robson
Chris Gregg QPM
Professor Patricia Wiltshire
Professor Gisli Gudjonsson

Contents

Introduction

A man runs down a dark alleyway, the sound of his footsteps echoing from the damp stone walls. As the camera pans in, we can see blood on his hands and on the front of his hooded jacket. Most of his face is hidden. But as he emerges from the shadows on to the dimly lit street he turns his head, and we catch a glimpse of what appear to be three scratch marks on his left cheek.

Cut to a forensic laboratory, where a scientist has just matched the sole of a trainer seized from a suspect's flat with the bloody footwear marks she had lifted earlier that morning from the floor of the kitchen where the terrible crime took place. 'If I can get a DNA sample from the scrapings taken from under the victim's fingernails,' she says, focusing the microscope with her own slender fingers, 'we might be able to identify the murderer before the end of the day.'

Typical scenes, perhaps, from one of the many fictionalised versions of forensic science that feature in some entertaining programmes on TV. But I think that *real* forensics is much more interesting and I hope that, after reading this book, you'll tend to agree.

My first book, *When the Dogs Don't Bark*, told the story of my professional career, initially as a forensic biologist with the Home Office Forensic Science Service, and then as a founder or co-founder of forensic companies, when I also specialised particularly in cold-case investigations.

During those years, I have been privileged to work with some of the most talented and inspirational forensic scientists in the UK. And *How to Solve a Crime* considers a much broader range of forensic expertise as I have tried to tell aspects of *their* stories, mixed with my own experiences, in an effort to present forensic science in its true light.

Because forensics can involve anything and everything encountered in everyday life, attempting to cover every aspect of it would be a very tall order. So I have tried instead to give a flavour of its richness and variety, and to counteract the notion that it is all about crime scene investigation (CSI). It's true that the crime scene is where most forensic science begins. But although CSI is certainly very important, it generally constitutes only part of the job of a forensic scientist.

The next stage in the process takes place in the laboratory, where items and samples from the crime scene and elsewhere are examined and tested, and the results are evaluated in the context of the specific circumstances of the case in hand. This, in turn, usually leads to the courtroom, where these results are presented as evidence for the judge and jury to consider.

While writing this book, I was aware that it mustn't end up being less about 'how to solve' than 'how to get away with' crime! Another thought that kept coming to the forefront of my mind was that there are two main things preventing us today from being able to solve virtually every crime. The first is error due to inexperience or lack of appropriate forensic skills. The second is the lack of sufficient funds being spent on collecting and investigating the evidence that *is* there somewhere, just waiting to be found.

'Smash and grab forensics' is no way to get to the bottom of a really complex case. Rather, it requires a combination of innovative approaches, laser-like observation, and testing carried out with surgical precision by dedicated and experienced forensic scientists to help to identify and convict the guilty and exonerate the innocent. Indeed, the contribution forensic science can make to the delivery of justice would be beyond the wildest imaginings of French criminologist Edmond Locard when he developed his principle of 'every contact leaves a trace' more than a hundred years ago. But he was spot on, as we have been able to prove time and time again.

Another reality that might not be apparent from watching TV programmes is that forensic scientists often don't know the outcomes of the cases they work on. This is because some of the many cases we deal with don't go to court until months, even years later, and we are not always called to give evidence when they do. Also, for someone to be convicted of a crime, it is usually necessary to have more than one type of evidence to link them with it. But I hope that the cases and details I have included at least give an idea of what forensic scientists actually do, and why they find the work so satisfying . . . most of the time.

I am very grateful to all the friends and colleagues (listed in the Acknowledgements) who shared their knowledge and experiences and who provided details of some of the case studies included.

Angela Gallop CBE, 2022

I

What insects can tell us about crime

One day, the fully clothed body of a farmer was found at the side of a road. The numerous wounds on his head appeared to have been inflicted with a sickle, and it was thought at first that he had been killed during the course of a robbery. But when it became apparent that no personal effects were missing from the body, the farmer's wife was questioned about any possible enemies he might have had. Although there were none that she could think of, she did give the investigator the name of a man who had recently asked to borrow money from her husband, but didn't get it.

Then the investigator, a man called Sung Tz'u, gathered together the men of the village and told them to place their sickles on the ground in front of them. It was a hot day, and Sung Tz'u waited and watched as flies began to alight on just one of the seventy or more curved-bladed implements.

The killing of the farmer occurred in rural China in the thirteenth century, and the murder – which was described in a book entitled *The Washing Away of Wrongs*,* written by Sung Tz'u and printed in 1247 – is generally recognised as being the first recorded case to involve forensic entomology. Sung Tz'u might not have been aware at the time that flies and other insects have sensory cells on their antennae that give

* Published in translation in 1981 by University of Michigan Press.

them an acute sense of smell and enable them to detect the odour of a body within minutes of death. What he obviously did know, however, was that the flies would be attracted to traces of blood on the sickle that had been used by the killer. And when faced with the evidence, the man who had tried to borrow money from the deceased farmer confessed to his murder.

From Greek mythology to the Renaissance paintings of the fifteenth century, flies have long been a symbol of death, the devil and decay. People have also been aware for many years of the value of information provided by insects in the forensic context. But it wasn't until the mid-1800s that insects began to be associated with murder in the West.

What is known today as forensic entomology is the study of insects and other invertebrate animals that are found on or around decomposing bodies or in other locations where these have been. One of the first forensic entomologists in Europe was a French physician called Louis Bergeret, who performed an autopsy in 1850 on the mummified body of a baby that had been found behind a fireplace in a flat.

What Bergeret discovered in several cavities of the baby's body were numerous empty larval skins – known as puparia, and cast off by pupae as they metamorphose to become adults – of the flesh fly species *Musca carnaria*. It was likely that the eggs from which the larvae had emerged had been laid shortly after death, and that the adults of this particular species would have developed the following year. Taking those facts into account, together with the natural history of the clothes-moth larvae that had also infested the mummified body, Bergeret concluded that death had occurred two years before it was found. It turned out that four families had rented the flat during the previous three years. And after three of them had been eliminated as suspects, one couple was arrested and ultimately convicted of the child's murder.

Forensic entomology is often used today to help estimate the time since death – also known as the post-mortem interval (PMI). What is actually being estimated is the time since colonisation by the insects, and as this will have occurred after death itself, when the body started to decompose, it provides only a minimum PMI. But when considered in conjunction with the maximum time since death – which is based on when the person was last seen alive – an estimate can be made of the window of time within which that person must have died.

The development of insects that metamorphose includes four distinct phases: egg, larva (called a maggot when the larva is a house fly or similar species), pupa and adult. If a body is outside and easily accessible, flies and other insects attracted by the smell will arrive in a sequence that reflects the state of decomposition. Each phase of insect development is also temperature dependent. So it is possible to gauge the time since death by examining the stage of development of specific types of insects on a corpse and ascertaining – from meteorological records, where necessary – the prevailing temperature when the insects developped.

One of the first recorded cases in the UK to have been solved on the basis of forensic entomology involved the murder of two women in 1935.

When the remains of the women's bodies were found near a stream in a ravine in Dumfriesshire in Scotland, they were identified as Isabella Kerr and Mary Rogerson. Isabella was the wife of a respected doctor called Buck Ruxton; Mary was their maid at their home in Lancaster, where the couple lived with their three children.

Maggots that were collected from the women's remains were examined at a laboratory at the University of Edinburgh, where they were identified as being between twelve and fourteen days old and from the blow-fly species. Having established that the bodies must have been in the location in which they were found for at least that length of time, suspicion fell on Dr Ruxton.

The evidence that seemed to implicate the doctor in the deaths of the two women included the skilful way in which the bodies had been dismembered – which might have been accounted for by his knowledge of anatomy. Also, the woman who cleaned the couple's house reported the presence of bloodstains and a horrible smell at the relevant time, and that the doctor had had a cut on his hand. And although the bodies were found in Dumfriesshire, about a hundred miles (160 km) away from their home in Lancaster, parts of them were wrapped in an edition of a newspaper that was only circulated in the Lancaster area. In the end, the evidence against Ruxton was overwhelming, and after being found guilty of murdering Isabella and Mary, he was hanged in 1936.

Forensic entomology can sometimes also provide an insight into the cause of death, the way in which someone died, and possibly the geographical area in which a body was kept before it was discovered. If a body has been moved, a forensic entomologist may be able to identify from the species of insects present where it was when the processes of decomposition and colonisation began.

The introduction of DNA profiling in the late 1980s provided another potentially reliable and durable source of insect-related forensic evidence, as the human DNA ingested by fly larvae when they feed off a decomposing cadaver can even be found in puparia. And seventy years after the murders of Isabella Kerr and Mary Rogerson, it was entomological evidence from puparia and dead flies that helped to identify the killer of 27-year-old mother of three Chantel Taylor.

Just over a year after Chantel had been reported missing from her home in Birkenhead in April 2004, there was an arson attack on a mosque in the town. DNA on clothing found near the mosque gave a match on the National DNA Database to a local man called Stephen Wynne.

When arrested, Wynne admitted to a charge of arson. And it was during a subsequent search of his house that a poem was discovered, which mentioned a 'junkie whore' ending up dead and DNA evidence waiting to be found. The original police investigation into the death of Chantel Taylor had high-lighted her violent partner as the only credible suspect. But when Wynne was questioned about the poem, he admitted to having murdered Chantel with a cleaver.

According to Wynne, he had picked Chantel up on the day she went missing and taken her to his home, where they had drunk alcohol, smoked cannabis and snorted cocaine. The next thing he remembered was coming round to find himself lying on the bathroom floor, surrounded by and covered 'from head to toe' with blood. The cleaver and Chantel's severed head and arms were lying beside her body in the bath. But Wynne claimed to have no memory of attacking her.

What he did remember, however, was transferring the unwrapped body parts to an old water tank in the loft. He had then put his clothing and Chantel's in two bin bags in the backyard of his house, together with a block of concrete in which he said he had encased the cleaver, before scrubbing the bathroom with bleach, and cleaning and painting the main bedroom. According to Wynne, two weeks after he had killed Chantel, he took her body parts out of the loft and disposed of them at several sites in the surrounding Wirral Peninsula. But although they were never found at the sites he identified, the bin bags and concrete block *were* discovered in his back-yard, as he described.

The fact that Chantel had had a previous run-in with the law meant that her DNA profile was on the National DNA Database. And when a DNA profile obtained from the blood on two extensively bloodstained shirts found in the bin bags was loaded on to the database, it was found to be a match for her.

Although Stephen Wynne was the primary suspect, his version of events still needed to be corroborated – or refuted – by solid evidence. So forensic investigators conducted a detailed examination of his house.

If his claim was true and he had carried Chantel's dismembered and unwrapped body from the bath to the loft, it was extremely unlikely that even rigorous and repeated cleaning would have removed every last trace of blood. And although there was no visible blood in the bathroom, when the carpet was pulled up and the bath panel removed, chemical screening tests gave a positive reaction for blood, which DNA analysis showed to be a match for Wynne himself. There were no visible bloodstains in the bedroom either. But again, when the carpet was lifted, blood was found on the floorboards and on the wooden joists beneath them, which DNA testing showed this time to be a match for Chantel.

No blood or body tissue was either visible or detected by chemical screening anywhere in the loft, where Wynne claimed he had kept the body before disposing of it. What the scientists did discover, however, were numerous adult flies and empty puparia on the floor, as well as hundreds more puparia under the plastic sheeting that covered a disused water tank.

Back at the laboratory, forensic entomologist Dr Samantha Pickles identified the pupae, puparia and adult flies as belonging to species of flesh flies, blow flies, house flies, lesser house flies and scuttle flies. Taking into account their presence in such large numbers and in such a variety of species, together with the fact that the pupae would have continued to develop to adults after their source of food had been removed, it seemed likely that the infestation had occurred and ended in the loft. This meant that it was also likely that the body parts

– if, indeed, that *was* what the insects had been feeding off – had been there for some time.

Toxicological testing of the puparia, led by Dr Alex Allan, revealed the presence of the heroin metabolite morphine, which suggested that the larvae had either fed on or passed through some substance that contained it. The fact that Chantel was known to have been a heroin addict added some significance to this finding. Also, DNA profiling from the puparia detected some DNA components that matched hers, as well as some that did not. So although the number of DNA contributors could not be established, it was *possible* that Chantel was one of them.

Meanwhile, the concrete block from Wynne's backyard had been broken open and found to contain a cleaver, saw blade and kitchen knife, none of which had any traces of blood, flesh, hair or textile fibres on them. And although DNA was found on the cleaver, it was not possible to confirm that any of it had come from the suspect or the victim. However, some blood spots on bedding found in the bin bags did provide a DNA match with Chantel, as did the DNA profile obtained from some fragments of bone whose appearance indicated that they were likely to be human.

There was nothing to implicate the original suspect – Chantel's apparently violent partner – in her killing and the disposal of her body. By contrast, various strands of the forensic evidence suggested that she could have been in the bedroom at Wynne's house, and that her body could have been stored in the loft there for a period of time. But while some aspects of the evidence supported Wynne's version of events, there was nothing to support his claim that Chantel had been in the bath, bleeding heavily, before being transferred to the loft, unwrapped and dripping blood. In the end though, when Stephen Wynne appeared before a judge at Liverpool Crown Court in January 2006, he unexpectedly pleaded guilty to the murder.

With his memory having apparently been restored, Wynne claimed that he and Chantel had shared drugs and alcohol before having sex in his bedroom. Then, on noticing that a bag of heroin had gone missing, and seeing it partially concealed under the top Chantel was wearing, an altercation had occurred during which he struck her neck with a cleaver. Bleeding heavily, Chantel had fallen on the floor at the foot of the bed. This is where, according to Wynne, he had left her for some time before dismembering her body and transferring the various body parts to the loft, where they remained until he disposed of them elsewhere.

Following a trial – and in the absence of a body, which has still not been found – Stephen Wynne was convicted of the murder of Chantel Taylor and sentenced to life in prison.

Insects have long been used to indicate time since death. But, as with so many other tools in the forensic scientist's armoury, they can sometimes provide much more subtle information – when a body has been moved, for example, or even, as in the case of Chantel Taylor, when a crime is suspected for some reason but no body has been found.

2

No body, no crime?

Contrary to what some people might believe, absence of a body does not equate to absence of evidence. So although absence of a body can certainly be a complicating factor in cases of suspected murder, it is often still possible to convict – or acquit – a particular suspect, as happened when a doctor called Hassan Al-Shatanawi was accused of murdering his wife in 1993.

Laura Al-Shatanawi had been missing from the couple's home in County Durham for more than three weeks by the time her husband went to the police. The reason he hadn't been unduly worried at first, he explained, was because he assumed she had gone on a trip she had been talking about taking.

I don't know whether the police already considered Al-Shatanawi to be a suspect in his wife's disappearance *before* he appeared on television to plead with her to come home. But they must certainly have done so after someone responded to the TV appeal saying that Hassan Al-Shatanawi had paid him £10 to burn a virtually new shed. Apparently, the shed had only very recently been erected on Al-Shatanawi's allotment. And fortuitously, as it turned out, instead of burning it as instructed, the man who contacted the police had actually sold it to a friend.

When scenes of crime officers and forensic scientists examined the shed, they found that an area of the surface of the floor measuring approximately three by two feet (0.9 x 0.6 m) appeared to have been cut or gouged away with a chisel or similar tool. Even more interesting were some small stains discovered on the edges of some of the floorboards in the damaged area, which tests proved to be blood mixed with, or possibly overlain by, a creosote-like wood preservative.

At first, traditional blood-grouping tests carried out at the Home Office Forensic Science Service (FSS) laboratory at Wetherby indicated that the blood in the shed could have come from Hassan Al-Shatanawi himself. However, this possibility was subsequently ruled out by DNA tests. (At that time – 1993 – the two types of test were often used in parallel, until DNA took over completely.) With Laura still missing, there were no samples of *her* blood available for analysis, but her medical records showed that she belonged to group B in the ABO blood-grouping system. This information, together with analysis of blood from her father, brother and son, indicated that the blood in the shed could have been hers.

Tests that were carried out on the saliva on the back of a stamp affixed to a postcard that Laura had sent to her parents while she was on holiday in Malta some years earlier indicated that the blood in the shed could have come from the person who had licked the stamp. But when saliva from where the stamp had been on another envelope sent by Laura a year later was tested, the results were different: it could have been Hassan's, but it could not have come from the same person whose blood was in the shed. So either Hassan had licked the stamp for Laura, or the blood on the floorboards wasn't hers at all.

After being employed by Hassan's defence solicitor, I visited the laboratory at Wetherby to examine some of the evidence. Having previously worked at the lab myself, I knew the scientists there very well. But checking their work on behalf of the defence was slightly different from working *with* them. In my early days as a 'defence expert', and before my colleagues and I became used to my rather different role, it used to feel like doing two jobs at once. One of those jobs was all about putting the scientist(s) who conducted the original work at their ease and reassuring them that I wasn't there to try to catch them out. The other involved reviewing the detail of what they'd done and found, so that I could work out what it might mean in terms of the case against the defendant and advise the solicitor accordingly.

One of the things I did while I was at the laboratory in Wetherby on that occasion was to stack the floorboards that had been removed from the shed in the same order they had been in while on the shed floor, to get an idea of the distribution of the blood on them. What I discovered was that some of the stains on the edge of one floorboard corresponded to those on its neighbour. This seemed to confirm that the blood had dripped between the two floorboards *after* the floor had been assembled, and that there had originally been substantial quantities of blood on their upper surfaces. Again though, without authentic reference samples, it wasn't possible to say how likely it was that the blood was Laura's.

None of the numerous tools that had been taken from the couple's house and tested during the original investigation could have been the chisel or similar implement that had been used to remove the surface of the floorboards. And although four human hairs recovered from the floor of the shed were generally similar in colour and microscopic appearance to hairs taken from Laura's hairbrush, they provided only a weak link with her in particular.

When the case went to court, the evidence against Hassan Al-Shatanawi included the hairs and the relatively large amount of blood that could have come from his wife and was found on the floor of the shed he owned at the time of her disappearance. On the other side of the argument were concerns about the lack of proper reference samples from Laura, the quality of some of the DNA results, and the statistical treatment of others. Apparently, however, the former outweighed the latter, and after being found guilty of murder, Hassan Al-Shatanawi was sentenced to life in prison. Laura's body has never been found.

It was forensic anthropology that helped to solve a case of suspected murder that occurred in 2004, when the only part of the victim's body that was found was a single fragment of bone.

When 55-year-old Margaret Gardiner's husband, John, reported his wife missing to the police, he claimed that the last time he had seen her was before she left their home in Helensburgh in Scotland to travel to London to visit their children. Following his arrest shortly afterwards, John Gardiner told his daughter part of the story of what had happened, before providing a statement to the police.

What Gardiner claimed was that he and his wife had argued while she was making a sandwich at lunchtime. When she turned on him during their altercation, he thought she was holding a knife in her hand. So he pushed her, and she fell down the kitchen steps, hitting her head in the process. Realising that she was dead, Gardiner wrapped her body in a towel and put it in the bath, which is where it remained until around two o'clock in the morning, when he transferred it to a polythene sheet, drove to a bridge in Dumbarton and dropped it in the River Leven. Then he drove home, washed out the bath, cleaned the polythene sheet and threw it in the bin, and washed the towel and his own bloodstained clothing in the washing machine.

No body (nor any human remains) was found in the river when it was dredged and searched by divers. And according to an expert in coastal oceanography, it was likely to have become trapped in the dense marshes at the river estuary.

When the couple's house was examined by forensic scientists, they found evidence of blood and a fragment of a tooth in the waste pipe of the bath. But it was a fragment of bone retrieved from the filter section of the washing machine that proved to be the key evidence.

Leading anthropologist Professor Sue Black was able to identify the fragment of bone as coming from a specific area of the sphenoid bone from a human skull. When it was examined by pathologist Dr Marjorie Turner, she made the point that it indicated a forceful injury. And when DNA was extracted from it, it proved to match Margaret Gardiner's DNA.

In September 2005, John Gardiner was found guilty of culpable homicide and of perverting the course of justice by hiding his wife's body. He was sentenced to six years in prison for each offence – subsequently reduced on appeal to a total of nine years – and was released in 2011.

When the body of a murder victim is found, there is always some type of evidence on it. Some of this will be clearly visible, such as wounds inflicted by knives, guns, blunt instruments or ligatures. Some of it may be more difficult to visualise, or even invisible to the naked eye, such as textile fibres, hairs and traces of body fluids from which DNA profiles can potentially be obtained. Sometimes, though, when no body has been found, and there is apparently only circumstantial evidence to indicate that a crime has taken place, other types of evidence have to be looked for, and other specialisms of forensic science may become involved in the investigation. As the cases described above illustrate, however, it would be a mistake for anyone who has committed a murder to think that disposing of the body will destroy all the evidence that could be used to identify them.

3

Blood: patterns and trails

It was my first day in my first job and I'd arrived early at the FSS facility in Harrogate, where I would be working as a higher scientific officer. After being shown upstairs to the biology laboratories in what used to be a large, suburban house, I was sitting on a stool, waiting for someone else to turn up, when I noticed some bloodstained items of clothing hanging from a washing line that was suspended across one corner of the room.

It was 1974, and there were few health and safety regulations in place. In fact, my own blood now runs cold when I think about the risks we took in those relatively early years, when testing for blood and semen, for example, involved using chemicals in the open laboratory that were subsequently proved to be carcinogenic. Or the distinctive taste of iron as puffs of blood dust were scattered into the air whenever we examined heavily bloodstained items. Later on, the drying of clothing, bedding etc. began to be restricted to fume cupboards. But although it was definitely a step in the right direction, these weren't really large enough to do an efficient job, and we ended up building proper drying rooms into the new laboratories we moved into at Wetherby in 1977, when the FSS labs in Harrogate and Newcastle were merged.

The rise in the use of forensic science that occurred during the 1970s was a reflection of advances in technology, and the

Home Office was investing large sums of money in new laboratories and employing more scientists. That expenditure was reduced a bit when subsequent labs were built at Huntingdon and Chepstow. But no expense was spared for that first new lab at Wetherby, which had wide corridors and even a bar! In fact, most of the labs had bars in those days. I thought it was very odd at the time, and it seems even odder when I look back on it with today's perspective.

I remained at Wetherby until 1981, then moved to the FSS lab at Aldermaston, which is where I worked until I left the FSS altogether in 1985 to set up my own company. I was married to a fellow forensic scientist by that time, and my husband eventually joined me at the new company, which I called Forensic Access. But for the first eighteen months I worked alone in a small room in our house in Newbury, in Berkshire.

It was in the very early days of DNA profiling, so I didn't need any of the high-tech equipment that would become necessary a few years later. In any event, my new role mostly involved checking the work of others, which meant that the emphasis was firmly on review rather than primary analysis. So I simply converted a room into an office, bought a reconditioned comparison microscope, some electrophoresis equipment, a small fridge for the chemicals I needed in order to do a bit of blood-grouping and textile-fibre analysis, and a state-of-the-art – at the time! – BBC Master home computer.

The reason I started Forensic Access was to try to redress the balance – which at that time was tipped very firmly in favour of the prosecution in almost all criminal cases – by providing second-opinion forensic services for the defence. So once my own 'home office' was set up, I started looking for clients.

One of the ways in which we linked suspects to crimes in those days was by using the presence of various forms of the same chemical substances in the blood, in the process known as blood grouping. Each blood-group system had advantages and disadvantages. For example, the ABO system was based on different antigens, and although it was relatively undiscriminating, it could be used with saliva and semen as well as blood itself, and lasted quite a long time after the body fluid had been shed. The PGM system, on the other hand, was based on different forms of the enzyme phosphoglucomutase; it was much more discriminating than ABO, and also worked on semen, but only lasted for about six weeks.

Today, it is the DNA in blood and other body fluids and tissues that makes it potentially useful in solving crime. And since DNA profiling became a regular tool in the forensic scientist's armoury in the late 1980s/early 1990s, the techniques involved have become increasingly sophisticated. With blood grouping, it was usually only possible to say, at best, that there was a one in a few thousand chance of a particular blood sample having come from someone other than the suspect or victim. With DNA profiling, that chance will be nearer one in a billion – which makes blood a more powerful form of evidence than ever.

However, DNA is only half the story. It can tell you from whom the blood, semen or saliva etc. could or could not have come, sometimes with a high degree of certainty. But it can't tell you anything about the sort of activity that gave rise to it. For this, you need to analyse the pattern(s) the bloodstaining forms. Blood pattern analysis can also be useful, for example, if there are two or more conflicting explanations of an incident, when it can sometimes help to indicate which version of events is more likely to be true.

In one case I became involved with at the request of the defendant's solicitor, it was alleged by the prosecution that John Barclay had carried out a severe and sustained assault on

Patrick Lewis* in a street in London, during which he had stamped repeatedly on Lewis's head and neck.

The defendant admitted to having been involved in a fight, but claimed merely to have been defending himself after Lewis had sprayed him in the face with CS gas. And although Barclay denied having stamped on Lewis, he did admit to pushing him to the ground with his right foot to prevent the alleged victim renewing his attack on *him*.

When the case was examined at the Metropolitan Police Forensic Science Laboratory (MPFSL), the scientist focused on examining Barclay's clothing for any blood that could have come from Lewis. Her findings included three areas of blood-staining on the uppers and sole of Barclay's right shoe, as well as some small spots and splashes of blood on the front of it, which tests showed could have come from Lewis but not from Barclay himself. The distribution of the blood was reported as being 'strongly indicative' of the wearer stamping on a heavily bloodstained surface.

When I visited the MPFSL to speak to the scientist and examine the items myself, I found several types of bloodstain as reported. Also, the bloodstaining on Barclay's right shoe included the most important characteristic elements of stamp-ing into wet blood. So if Barclay's claim was true, and he had knocked Lewis to the ground by pushing him in the chest with his foot, the bloodstaining could only be explained if Lewis's clothing had been sodden with blood at the time. One might also expect Lewis to have sustained some injury from the force of the blow.

There is no means of establishing how many times such 'stamping' would have to have occurred to account for the bloodstaining on Barclay's clothes. There must have been a minimum of two blows, however – the first to break the skin

* Not their real names.

and start the blood flow, and the second (and any subsequent blows) to splash and spatter blood on to the shoe. So it was difficult to see how such a pattern could have been produced merely by Barclay pushing Lewis to the ground with his foot. Therefore, on this occasion, rather than being able to provide any additional insights for Barclay's legal team to use in his defence, my observations appeared to be more supportive of the prosecution's case. But at least the defence team knew where they were.

In conjunction with the injuries a victim has sustained, blood pattern analysis can provide the scientist with an idea of what happened at a crime scene and, in some cases, with quite a detailed sequence of events. In particularly violent cases, it can also indicate whether any of the blood might alternatively have come from an offender, which is a very useful starting point for obtaining their DNA profile, from which they might then be identified.

Blood patterns are formed whenever blood is spilled, and it is the nature and distribution of the different elements of such a pattern that are important. For instance, smears and smudges of blood result from contact between two surfaces, at least one of which has some wet bloodstaining on it. If the staining is in the form of a print, it may tell you that it has been made by a bloodstained finger or the sole of a shoe, for example. Sometimes, there is also a directional component to the appearance of a smear. Splashed or spattered stains – as in the case described above – arise when wet blood is subjected to some sort of force that causes it to split up into droplets and fan out away from the point at which the force was applied.

The greater the speed of impact, the smaller are the individual droplets of blood produced. For example, the blood pattern resulting from being stabbed with a knife or shaking blood-covered hands will look very different from that due to being struck with a fist or hammer, which is different again from that resulting from having been shot with a gun. Then there are blood films, which result from contact with a substantial quantity of wet blood, causing it to flow over a surface in a continuous layer.

There are several chemicals that are used to help locate blood at crime scenes and other places of potential significance, such as the houses and vehicles of suspects, on their clothing and on anything that might have been used for a weapon. What all these chemicals have in common is that they exist in two different states, one colourless and the other brightly coloured. Transition from the former to the latter occurs in the presence of blood – or, rather, in the presence of the oxygen that is released when blood reacts with hydrogen peroxide (bleach), which is also included in the test.

A positive reaction to a chemical test for blood is therefore usually indicated by a change in the colour of the reagent, which may be from colourless to pink or blue-green, depending on which test is used. For the test that involves the use of the chemical luminol, however, a positive reaction is indicated not by a colour change but by chemiluminescence – in other words, it causes the blood to 'glow in the dark'. This can also give some indication of the size, shape and density of stains and their distribution, which are important for working out how they were formed and therefore what activities might have taken place to produce them.

Although luminol is extremely sensitive, it is presumptive only – like the colour tests – and therefore requires follow-up with a confirmatory test. It does, however, have the disadvantage of having to be performed entirely in the dark, which is one of the reasons why it fell out of favour when colour-change tests were developed in the mid-1900s. It has been re-introduced in recent years, but only in specific circumstances, such as where it is suspected that a clean-up has been attempted, and to detect blood on 'difficult' surfaces, such as drag marks or the details of a bloody shoeprint on a dark-coloured, heavily patterned carpet.

I first used luminol myself in 1989, when I was asked to provide a second opinion in an Italian murder case in which the results of luminol tests were being used as part of the prosecution's case against a defendant called Massimo Carlotto.

In January 1976, Carlotto was a student in Padua, northern Italy, when he claimed to have been passing a building and heard someone crying out for help. His sister had a flat on the ground floor of the building, but was away at the time. So, finding the door to the street unlocked, he went to the upstairs flat, where the voice seemed to be coming from.

On the floor of a built-in wardrobe, he found a young woman, lying naked and covered in blood. Bending down on her left side, he was reaching across her body towards her face when she raised her right arm, then let it fall to the floor and closed her eyes. Thinking she was dead, Carlotto ran out of the flat and to the house of some friends, who advised him to report what had happened to the police. But as soon as he had done so, he was arrested and charged with the murder of 25-year-old Margherita Magello.

In 1978, after spending two years in detention, Carlotto was tried for murder, but acquitted due to lack of evidence. The following year, the Italian Ministry of Justice began appeal proceedings to try to have the original verdict over-turned. And when the case was heard by the Appeal Court in Venice, Carlotto was found guilty of murder and sentenced to eighteen years in prison. In fact, though, for reasons that aren't totally clear, he ended up living for a while in Mexico before being expelled from there in 1985, when he returned to Italy and was imprisoned.

It was when the Italian Supreme Court ordered a retrial in 1989 that I became involved in the case. And that's when I taught myself how to use the luminol test, which was regarded as being very old-fashioned and wasn't used in UK forensics at all at that time.

In order to be able to photograph the reaction of luminol in the dark, you had to set up a camera on a tripod, then position and focus it over the item so that you were ready to take a series of photographs as soon as you sprayed the chemical in the dark. Because the exposure time is so long, you then had to keep the camera very steady as the luminol fluoresced, particularly because having to repeat the process and spray the item again – possibly several times – risks the blood becoming more diffuse and starting to dissolve in the solution.

Part of the reason I had to experiment and do lots of practice with luminol for the Carlotto case was because the pathologist involved in the case had said that Carlotto's clothes were plastered in blood, and that once blood dries on an item it is absolutely fixed on it and never flakes off. In other words, the pattern and extent of bloodstaining on the items would reflect what they were like at the time of the incident. But, in fact, that isn't true. Blood powders as it dries, producing the little puffs of blood dust mentioned above when it is handled, the particles of which then settle and resettle well beyond the boundaries of the original bloodstain. Over the years, the clothes had been taken in and out of their bags and handled extensively on several occasions, providing lots of opportunity for the blood to become dispersed across them in this way and appear much more extensive than it had originally been. So when you then use luminol, anything can look as though it's plastered in blood.

I think the pathologist was getting confused by the fact that in blood grouping, the older the blood is, the more difficult it is to get it into solution so that you can then group it, particularly from some types of fabric. To illustrate the point, some of my experiments involved putting a small amount of blood on an item, then repeatedly putting the item in a bag and getting it out again, and showing how much more extensive the blood on it was at the end of the process than at the beginning. So I was also able to show that, because of its extreme sensitivity, combined with the way in which the items in the case had been handled over the years, the luminol results in this instance had given a completely misleading impression of the extent of bloodstaining on Carlotto's clothing. I believed that this bloodstaining was actually entirely consistent with his own account of events, and did not indicate – as suggested by the prosecution – that he had played any active role in attacking the victim.

Unfortunately, due to the fact that the Italian Legal Code in force at the time apparently provided grounds for exclusion, neither I nor the French forensic scientist who also attended the trial was allowed to give evidence in the court in Venice, and Massimo Carlotto was convicted. But three years later, following an international campaign for justice, he was pardoned by the President of Italy – and went on to be a successful crime writer.

It was a trail of blood that helped to identify one of the killers of city financier John Monckton, who lived with his wife and two daughters in Chelsea in west London.

At around 7.30 p.m. on 29 November 2004, John Monckton opened the front door of his house expecting to take delivery of a parcel. Realising immediately that something was wrong, he was trying to shut the door again when two men, one of whom was wearing a balaclava and holding a knife in each hand, managed to force their way in.

As John's wife, Homeyra, started up the stairs in an attempt to reach a panic button, she was stabbed twice in the back by one of the men, who demanded her jewellery. The last thing she saw before she blacked out was her husband defending himself against the other man. When she came round, the attackers were leaving and John was lying on the floor.

One of the couple's young daughters, who was upstairs when the break-in occurred, phoned the police. But 49-year-old John Monckton died shortly afterwards.

When forensic scientist Ed Jarman was called to the scene that night, he took numerous items and samples for analysis. Some of the samples were from the substantial amount of blood in the hallway, which continued in a trail for about 50 metres (55 yards) towards the King's Road. The blood leading out of the house had clearly dripped from a bleeding injury, and it provided the police with a useful line of investigation. Although DNA tests on samples from the trail also produced a full profile, it didn't match any of the profiles on the National DNA Database.

The police quickly identified two people of interest in connection with the case, the DNA of one of whom had not been loaded on to the database, as it should have been. But after the mistake was rectified, the DNA profile from the blood in the trail was found to match that of a man called Elliot White. And when two of six samples from inside the hallway of the house were also found to match White's DNA, it placed him firmly at the scene. (The DNA profile obtained from the rest of the blood in the hallway matched that of John Monckton.)

Apparently, after leaving the scene of the crime, White and the other assailant, Damien Hanson, had gone to White's home, where they had attempted to burn the clothes they had been wearing. But they set the fire too close to an outhouse, and when it shorted out the electrics, the fire brigade was alerted.

Among the items that were rescued from the fire were fragments of blood-soaked clothing and the soles of some shoes. And when these items were subsequently examined and analysed in the LGC Forensics laboratory at Culham, some of the blood gave a match for White's DNA, and some seemed to have come from Homeyra Monckton.

It turned out that during the struggle that ensued after the two suspects had forced their way into the house, John Monckton's hand had been held behind his back while Hanson stabbed him several times, and the blade of the knife had also penetrated White's arm. After stabbing Homeyra, the intruders had stolen a pair of earrings, two rings, a watch and a purse – all valued at just £4,000 – before fleeing from the house, with White leaving an incriminating trail of blood behind him.

At their trial in November 2005, White and Hanson blamed each other in what is known as a cut-throat defence. In the end though, Hanson was convicted of murder, attempted murder and robbery and was sentenced to a minimum of thirty-six years in prison, while White was sentenced to eighteen years for manslaughter, wounding with intent to cause grievous bodily harm and robbery.

There are two main aspects to blood evidence, which are equally important, depending on what question you are trying to answer. If you want to know from whom a sample of blood could or could not have come, it's all about the DNA – or, in the old days, the blood groups – it contains. If, on the other hand, you want to know what happened, then what's important are the patterns formed by the blood as it's shed from the victim's – and sometimes the suspect's – injuries on to clothing, weapons and other items or surfaces at the crime scene. Usually, however, both aspects are required.

4

Human prints and marks

Differences between fingerprints left by different people have been recognised for many years, but the person who is generally credited as being the first to use them to solve a crime is a Scottish doctor called Henry Faulds. In a letter to the journal *Nature* in 1880, Dr Faulds suggested that fingerprints found at the scene of a crime could positively identify the perpetrator. He then put his theory into practice in Tokyo – where he was working at the time – when the police there were investigating a burglary and found some fingerprints on a cup. Dr Faulds had a small experimental collection of fingerprints, and it was quite by chance that he discovered some that were identical to those on the cup. The matching prints had been taken from a servant working in a house nearby who, when questioned, confessed to the crime.

The case sparked a considerable amount of interest, and the first proper book on the subject – by the eminent scientist Dr (later Sir) Francis Galton – was published in 1892. The idea was picked up in Argentina by Juan Vucetich, who was a policeman in La Plata, and then in England by Edward Henry, who was to become head of Scotland Yard. Both men devised their own fingerprint classification systems in what was a critical first step to being able to analyse and compare prints. The system Edward Henry devised became the industry standard in the UK, and remained as such for many years.

It was the sequential use of radioactive sulphur dioxide followed by gentian violet dye to develop a fingerprint that proved useful in an appeal case we were asked to examine more than a hundred years after Dr Faulds' discovery.

Following the deaths of four soldiers in an Irish Republican Army (IRA) terrorist bombing at Hyde Park in July 1982, Gilbert (Danny) McNamee's fingerprint was found on electronic circuits that were linked to the attack. At his trial at the Old Bailey in 1987, McNamee denied having any connection with or sympathy for the IRA and claimed that he might have handled the circuits while employed on a previous job as an electronic engineer. But he was found guilty on all charges and sentenced to twenty-five years in prison.

Ten years later, the case was the subject of the Channel 4 programme *Trial and Error.* And in December 1998, after becoming the first case to be referred to the Court of Appeal by the recently established Criminal Cases Review Commission, McNamee's conviction was overturned.

There was also a forensic scientist involved for the defence, and the basis for the successful appeal was the fact that other, more prominent fingerprints had been found on the same circuits. These prints belonged to a known IRA bomb maker who, at the time of McNamee's original trial, was already serving a ten-year sentence for possession of explosives – which was evidence that had not been disclosed to the original trial judge.

Fingerprinting was discovered well before any forensic laboratories came into existence, and has therefore historically been conducted by the police. Otherwise, I'm sure fingerprints would have been regarded as just another – albeit very important – type of evidential mark dealt with in labs. However, forensic scientists have long been instrumental in helping to develop new techniques for locating and enhancing the prints, particularly in complex cases, to increase the amount of information available within the prints and thereby assist the police with their fingerprint-related investigations.

Fingerprints consist of a series of lines (or ridges) that arch, loop and whorl within the print, and it is these characteristics, and particularly variations in them, that define someone's fingerprint. A second level of detail that can be used in identification includes the position of individual microscopic sweat pores along the ridges. Fingerprints are actually made of the sweat that is secreted through these pores, mixed with oils and salt from the skin and other parts of the body that the hands may touch, as well as the environmental grime that collects on the skin's surface.

Because no two fingerprints made by different people have ever been found to match – even those of identical twins – they are thought to be unique to individual people, and to remain the same from birth to death. As with most things in forensic science, however, fingerprinting isn't that simple, particularly because many of the fingerprints that feature in crime are partial, smudged, overlaid or otherwise indistinct. Also, on many surfaces, they can be very difficult to see; these are known as latent prints.

Latent prints can be visualised using a wide variety of methods, which are chosen according to the type of surface you are dealing with – paper, plastic, glass etc. – and what they might have been made in – for example blood, ink or grease. These methods include the use of special lighting conditions or light of particular wavelengths, as well as physical methods such as gently brushing the surface with aluminium or other very fine powder. The powder sticks to the surface and improves the contrast between the print and its background, therefore making it more visible.

Other methods involve chemicals, notably ninhydrin, but also including, for example, gentian violet, physical developer and Superglue (which is particularly good for visualising prints on plastic). Some chemical methods – such as the radio-active sulphur method used in the McNamee appeal case – are highly specialised and only used at certain centres, whereas the use of others is more widespread. The different methods tend to be employed sequentially in a strict order of priority, to get the most information out of any prints detected.

The process of fingerprint identification currently used in most countries involves four steps: analysis, comparison, evaluation and verification (ACE-V). If no suspect has been identified, and therefore no comparison can be made with a fingerprint lifted from a crime scene, Automated Fingerprint Identification System (AFIS) technology is used to check the fingerprint under investigation against the databases that have been compiled over the years by police and other law-enforcement agencies around the world.

Despite the requirement for verification of the results – which involves someone different repeating the first three steps – the system is not infallible, and errors *can* occur. These may be due to poor technique or confirmation bias – for example if the scientist responsible for the verification part of the process is a colleague of the scientist whose work they are checking. As shown in studies conducted by the eminent UK cognitive psychologist Dr Itiel Dror, this type of error can also occur if an examiner is aware of the details of a case, which may influence their decision-making process.

One such error was made following the terrorist bombings of four crowded commuter trains in Madrid in March 2004, which killed 191 people and injured around 2,000.

During a search of the surrounding area, investigators found a plastic bag containing detonator caps and a single fingerprint. A few weeks later, the FBI arrested an Oregon lawyer called Brandon Mayfield, whom they claimed was a match for the fingerprint. But within days, Spanish police had arrested another suspect, an Algerian national whose fingerprint they believed was a 'better match' than Mayfield's, and who was subsequently charged with the offence.

The mistake that led to the wrongful arrest of Brandon Mayfield was made in an FBI fingerprint laboratory by the initial examiner. It was then corroborated by at least two investigators, as well as by an independent examiner working for the defence. So how could they all have got it so wrong? Part of the answer seems to be that the fingerprints of the two men were very similar, and the FBI examiners, at least, already believed Mayfield to be the source – which highlights one of the problems inherent in having hunches and 'knowing' things.

Another example of the mistaken attribution of a fingerprint – and possibly also an element of confirmation bias – occurred in the investigation of a case involving the murder of a woman called Marion Ross in her home in Kilmarnock, Scotland, in 1997.

Shirley McKie was a detective constable in Strathclyde Police at the time, and her thumbprint was supposedly found on the bathroom door at the crime scene. Although DC McKie had been among the police officers on duty *outside* the house following the discovery of the body, she insisted that she had not been *inside* it, and therefore that the thumbprint could not be hers. But four fingerprint experts working for the Scottish Criminal Record Office (SCRO) insisted otherwise. And in 1999, after being suspended from duty and then sacked, DC McKie was arrested and charged with perjury.

At her trial, three SCRO experts reiterated their conclusion that the thumbprint found at the crime scene was that of DC McKie. However, two American fingerprint experts who also gave evidence stated that the differences between the defendant's thumbprint and the print on the bathroom door were so obvious that it had taken them only seconds to identify them. So DC McKie was acquitted.

Meanwhile, after being tried and found guilty of murdering Marion Ross – based largely on fingerprint evidence – a man called David Asbury was sentenced to life in prison. Three years later, his conviction was quashed at appeal when the judges accepted that the fingerprint evidence was, in general, unreliable.

As a result of the McKie/Asbury case, the eminent QC Michael Mansfield called for more quality control to be applied to fingerprinting, and for all previous SCRO cases that had relied on fingerprint evidence to be reviewed. The public inquiry that followed highlighted weaknesses in the SCRO's fingerprint services and found that the erroneous identification of Shirley McKie's fingerprint was due to 'human error'. The report also made numerous recommendations, including the need for all fingerprint evidence to be regarded as opinion rather than fact.

This highlights a common problem with the general perception of scientific evidence as an especially pure form of evidence capable of providing definitive answers that leave little scope for debate. But it all depends on what questions you ask, on the specific circumstances of individual cases, and on how much information you have about them. So, while scientific evidence may be born of fact, it is always tempered by context.

Of course, it isn't just the fingerprints that are left behind at crime scenes that help in the forensic investigations of crimes. There are many other types of marks and prints, including those made by lips and ears. But, these days, they are all really only useful as potential sources of DNA.

Another type of mark that can help to identify the perpetrators of crimes, as well as the nature of an attack, is bite marks that have been left on a victim or in food at a crime scene. Bite marks are found in a variety of different types of assault, including, particularly, sexual offences, child abuse and homicides.

Human bite marks are typically oval or circular in shape. Depending on the severity of the bite, they vary from suction marks – often referred to as love bites or hickeys – to complete disruption or tearing off (avulsion) of the tissue. Between these two extremes is obvious bruising with several areas of laceration and/or incision that represent the positions of individual teeth as they sank into the flesh. In the most extreme cases, parts of the ear or nose can be bitten off.

As with fingerprints, no two people have identical teeth, and individuality may be enhanced by factors such as malformed, chipped or missing teeth. This means that if a bite mark is sufficiently clear, it can be possible to link it – to some degree or another – with a specific person. This requires precise photography of the marks with appropriate scales, which can be difficult to achieve, depending on which part of the victim's body is affected. Sometimes, it may be necessary to take more than one set of photographs as the injury gradually changes in appearance with healing. This may result in some features – such as the precise position of the biter's teeth – becoming clearer as initial swelling subsides.

The specialised form of dentistry known as forensic odontology relies on the facts that teeth – and the jaws in which they are set – are different in different people, and that they are incredibly hard. These differences reflect how they were formed and the relative space they have to occupy within the jaw, as well as the sorts of damage they have picked up in life, and how that damage has been dealt with. So identifications of victims of individual crimes or mass disasters are based on matching dental patterns with any previous X-rays, dental casts and written records, and also with photographs taken during the person's life.

As well as making casts of a suspect's teeth and bite, these are also made of the alleged victim's teeth if there is any possibility that the bite mark might have been self-inflicted. (In the latter circumstance, the bite would obviously have to be on a part of the body that the alleged victim can access.) These reference marks can then be compared with the crime mark on the victim's body, assisted by modern imaging techniques when required.

Sometimes, bite marks that are potentially relevant to a case are found in other items at the crime scene, such as apples, lumps of cheese and other foodstuffs. (It always amazes me that some criminals clearly feel compelled – and able – to eat during the commission of a crime.) These marks are treated generally in the same way as marks on a victim's body. If the foodstuff is perishable – as in the case of an apple – the marks will need to be recorded as soon as possible.

Bite marks are also routinely swabbed, as the biter's saliva may provide a good source of DNA. This would help to confirm that the mark was made by biting, and could provide a very strong link with the person responsible. In fact, the analysis of bite marks has largely been superseded – at least in terms of comparisons – by DNA in the saliva that often accompanies them. But they can prove extremely useful in indicating where saliva samples may be found for this purpose.

Bite marks are also a central feature of attacks by animals such as dogs. These are unlikely to be confused with human bite marks due to their different-shaped dental arches and dentition. They can produce very useful evidence in their own right, related to the nature and severity of an attack, and to the dog that might have been responsible.

There are also numerous other animals whose bite marks feature in forensic casework from time to time. For example, in two cases of damage that was initially thought to have been caused by humans, one turned out to be the result of rats biting through electric cables, while the other was caused by rabbits chewing on the protective sheathing around young saplings.

Just as fingerprints can be identified by the shape and pattern of their loops, whorls and arches, ear prints also have identifying characteristics, which include the length, width and shape of the outer ear and its constituent parts. Sometimes an ear print is found at the scene of a crime, imprinted during a struggle for instance, or where a perpetrator listened at a door or window by pressing an ear against it before breaking in.

The first reports of the use of ear prints to link people with places came from Switzerland in the mid-1960s. Since then, ear-print evidence has been used in a number of cases, notably in Holland and, to a lesser extent, the UK. There are severe limitations to the technique, however, and it has been shown in tests that it is possible for the same ear to leave significantly different prints, and for different ears to leave very similar prints. The reason for this is because the quality of the print depends on the nature of the contact between ear and surface. Relevant factors include how long the contact lasted, the extent to which the ear moved during the period of contact, and how greasy the ear might have been with natural oils and waxes. Also important are the surface on which the print was made, any environmental factors that may have altered it subsequently, and how the ear print was lifted from the surface.

A notable case involving ear prints was the murder in Huddersfield in 1996 of 94-year-old Dorothy Wood.

Dorothy's murderer had apparently left ear prints on the window of her downstairs bedroom, before climbing in and suffocating her with a pillow as she lay in bed. These ear prints formed a central plank of the evidence against Mark Dallagher at his trial two years later, when it was presented by Dutch police officer Cornelis Van Der Lugt. Van Der Lugt had specialised in ear-print analysis and had previously given evidence based on it in a number of other cases. At Dallagher's trial, he said that ear prints are unique and that he was convinced the prints in this case were made by the suspect. So Dallagher was convicted.

Eventually, having protested his innocence throughout, Mark Dallagher appealed against his conviction. At a retrial in 2003, DNA-profiling evidence was presented that proved the marks had been made by someone else. And after being freed on bail while his case was reviewed, he was finally acquitted in January 2004.

These days, although ear prints are regarded as interesting, it is recognised that they need to be far better understood, and reliable techniques for their analysis and comparison developed and properly validated, before they can ever be considered for use as evidence again.

Theoretically, any part of the human body can leave a mark when it comes into contact with another surface. From the forensic scientist's point of view, the most important type of human marks are undoubtedly fingerprints, due to the presence of sweat and the fine ridges on the undersides of fingers and palms, which leave distinctive and individualised prints on objects that have been handled and touched. But marks made by lips, teeth, feet and ears can also feature in forensic evidence, although sometimes less reliably.

5

Other marks and trails

Even criminals who think they have taken every precaution to cover their tracks are likely to leave some sort of mark, trace or trail behind them that can later provide evidence linking them to their crime. It was a footwear mark on some broken glass that helped to identify the suspect in one case we worked on in Manchester.

A scenes of crime officer had examined some business premises in Manchester the day after a burglary and the theft of some property. In his report, he stated that entry had been gained via a window and that a glass panel in a door to the offices had been broken. A pair of ankle boots was seized from the home of one of the suspects. When they were examined at the FSS laboratory at Chorley, the soles were found to have a complex pattern consisting of blocks with fine bars and circular studs, some of which were particularly characteristic. Also of interest were the wear and signs of damage on the treads of the boots, particularly on the left one, which exactly mirrored a footwear impression on the broken glass.

We were asked by the defendant's solicitor to check the forensic evidence related to the glass and footwear mark. So my colleague Dr Clive Candy made a series of test prints with the boots, which he compared with the photographs of the impressions on the glass. What he found was that the pattern on the left boot corresponded very closely with one of the test marks in terms of relative size, the spacing and shapes of the dots and circles, and the microscopic cuts and gouges resulting from wear and tear. All of this was compelling evidence in support of the prosecution's claim that the suspect had, indeed, been present at the offices when the glass panel was broken and the burglary occurred.

There is a wide variety of types of marks that criminals can leave behind them, which later provide evidence to connect them with their crimes, perhaps showing how they were committed and where best to take samples that might incriminate them. The most common of these are shoe marks, and the trails – often in blood – that can be left by an attacker as they flee the crime scene. There may be tyre marks on the bodies of hit-and-run victims or left behind on grass verges at crime scenes. Tool marks can be created when doors and windows are jemmied open as the prelude to theft and robbery, or on bullets as they are fired from a gun. The manufacturing marks that are left on small self-seal polythene bags used by drug dealers can link different seizures, both with each other and with the dealers themselves. And there is a whole variety of other marks that are specific to individual cases.

A trail might involve drugs being thrown out of car windows during a police chase in an attempt to get rid of the evidence before the car is finally stopped. It might be composed of abandoned clothing that has been scattered by fleeing offenders as they change their appearance from what eyewitnesses may describe. It could be flattened vegetation at an outdoor crime scene indicating the paths taken by an offender as they approached and left. Digital trails involving CCTV footage might show the movement of cars to and from a crime scene. Mobile-phone usage could indicate who was where and talking to whom at critical times. Or there may be digital evidence showing who had been hacking into company IT systems in preparation for attempts at blackmail or the theft of sensitive information. One example of a more unusual trail involved jewellery discarded in hedgerows by the serial killer John Cooper as he returned from an evening of burgling (see Chapter 8). But perhaps the most common types of trail involve blood dripping from offenders as they make their way out of crime scenes where they too were injured, and footwear marks made in victims' blood as offenders search other parts of crime scenes or make their getaway.

In fact, footwear marks can be composed of almost anything the offender may have trodden in, which, as well as blood, may include greasy deposits, soil and just general dirt. They can be found almost anywhere it is possible for someone to put their feet: in flowerbeds, for example; on windowsills if the perpetrator climbed into or out of the premises; on floors and on items that may be lying on a floor and that the perpetrator stood on; and on the clothing and bodies of victims if they have been stamped on.

A faint footwear mark, or even one that isn't visible to the naked eye at all, can be visualised or enhanced using a whole range of techniques, all of which are designed to provide better contrast between the mark and the surface on which it has been made. Depending on the circumstances, these techniques include oblique light, where shadows provide the contrast; powdering similar to the process used for fingerprints; and chemical reagents that react with substances in the mark.

Footwear marks made in blood are very common at scenes of violent assault. They can provide valuable information about the footwear itself, and about where the perpetrator went immediately after the attack, even after all visible signs of a blood trail have petered out. Of course, the blood – and, more particularly, the DNA it contains – can also provide very powerful additional evidence of a link between a shoe and a victim.

Test prints can be made by brushing a thin layer of – usually black – powder on to the sole of a shoe or boot and placing it in contact with a transparent sticky film. When the film is peeled off, a detailed print of the tread pattern is produced, which is stuck down on to a clear plastic sheet to protect it. The test print can then be laid on top of the footwear mark that has been photographed (with a scale) or lifted from the crime scene, or on a cast that has been made of it, so that the general size and pattern characteristics of the two can be directly compared.

Casts are made of footwear marks that are three-dimensional – because the shoe has sunk into the surface of soil in a flowerbed, for example. Plaster of Paris was originally used for this purpose, but has now been replaced by synthetic, more robust materials, usually of the sort used by dentists. Again, a scale is placed beside the cast before photographs are taken that can be used for comparison with any impressions of the tread patterns on the soles of shoes belonging to any suspects, and with manufacturers' and other databases.

The cuts and gouges on the soles of shoes and boots are unique, having been picked up randomly in the course of normal wear. So it is often possible to distinguish the impression left by the sole of one item of footwear from that left by another with a similar overall pattern but worn by someone else. In a clear shoeprint made on a relatively smooth surface, the cuts and gouges usually appear as distinct and characteristic breaks in the footwear mark. One of the best types of surface on which these fine details can be reproduced is the smooth surface of glass.

It was marks on a body that were at the centre of a case of suspected murder that my colleague Mike Jenkins worked on in the late 1990s. In oral evidence, the prosecution's forensic odontologist stated that he had compared some marks that were apparent in photographs taken of the deceased man's body with the handle of a vehicle jack and that, in his opinion, the marks had been produced by that handle or something identical to it.

When we were brought in by the defence, Mike examined the same photographs and two cabutans – a type of self-defence weapon that can be extended with a flick of the wrist to form a longer bar. As he explained in his report to the defendant's solicitor, the appearance of marks on the skin is influenced by numerous factors. These include the design and shape of the instrument or weapon used; the force and angle of impact; and the structure of the tissue and/or bone at the point of impact. The edge of the instrument as well as any grooves or ridges on it will also produce a pattern of bruising that will vary according to the force of the impact – from simple marks reflecting the pattern on the instrument with a light impact, to extensive bruising with little or no evidence of pattern with a heavier force. The fact that the body is contoured rather than a flat, non-distorting surface also means that any measurements of the patterns of marks etc. taken from photographs will not be indicative of the actual width and spacing of the features that make up those patterns on the instrument itself.

In this particular case, there were cuts and some relatively broad marks on the body that were thought to have been made by a knife and a baseball bat, respectively, as well as some marks that were in a closely spaced 'tramline' pattern.

Mike examined the photographs, the handle of the vehicle jack and the cabutans carefully, but wasn't able to take any measurements of the actual marks on the body. And while he concluded that the marks on the body *could* have been made by the hexagonal-shaped nut at one end of the handle, he was 'not entirely convinced' that this feature would necessarily have been present on the instrument responsible, which might, alternatively, have been one of the cabutans.

*   *   *

There is a very wide range of marks and trails that are of interest to forensic scientists, depending on the circumstances of individual cases. But while it's one thing to recognise the type of mark one is dealing with, it's quite another to identify a unique association with the specific item that made it. So it is important to examine, probe and test the evidence from every angle.

6

DNA profiling

Just as blood patterns can tell you what happened during an assault, DNA profiling can tell you who might have been involved, and the power of forensic science is to be able to combine information from both. But DNA profiling is a relatively expensive procedure, involving the use of some high-tech – and therefore high-cost – equipment. So the fact that you can sometimes work out the best place to take samples for DNA profiling by examining the blood patterns at a crime scene or on a suspect's or victim's clothing can prove very useful.

DNA profiling has been the most significant development in forensic science during the last fifty years. It has transformed the strength of the link between individual people and traces of saliva, semen, blood, skin flakes and other traces from people's bodies. And it has completely superseded blood grouping in terms of the analysis of body fluids.

Before the geneticist Professor Sir Alec Jeffreys developed a technique for DNA profiling and used it in a case for the first time in the mid-1980s, we all knew that people's individuality was coded in DNA and understood about heredity. We used to say that someone would eventually work out how to analyse DNA, or something directly related to it, and that it was only a matter of time before DNA analysis was introduced into forensic science generally. What we didn't know was when that would happen, or how. But we'd started storing evidential items and samples of stains for which we thought it might be useful in the freezers in our labs. So we were able to start testing them as soon as it came properly into use, and I can remember many cases over the years when we went back and looked at old samples. In fact, we're still doing it today, and there are many examples of cases for which blood grouping didn't reveal anything, but analysing DNA subsequently gave a result and helped to solve the case.

During the latter half of the 1980s, Alec Jeffreys had close links with a company called Cellmark, which was set up in 1987, the year after I started Forensic Access. The two companies were close geographically, and we used to do a lot of work with Cellmark, particularly involving screening tests to show where a semen stain on an item was strongest, and therefore where they might obtain the best results from DNA profiling. And it was because of that connection that Alec Jeffreys came to our lab at Culham, in Oxfordshire, one day in those early years to talk to the staff about DNA.

The DNA in each of us is the same throughout our body – in our blood, saliva and other body fluids, tissues, organs, and in the roots of our hairs. It can be detected on anything that someone has worn or handled and can last for decades, or even longer in the right (dry, cool) conditions. As the technology has advanced and the techniques have been refined, it has become possible for results to be obtained from traces of material so small that they aren't visible to the naked eye.

The technique of DNA profiling (originally also known as DNA fingerprinting) was used for the first time in a criminal context to help the police who were investigating the murders in Leicestershire of two fifteen-year-old girls – Lynda Mann in 1983 and Dawn Ashworth in 1986. The prime suspect in both cases was Richard Buckland, who was seventeen at the time of Dawn's death. But Buckland's DNA did not match the profile that had been obtained from the semen that stained the clothing of both girls.

Suspecting that a local man was responsible for the murders, the police carried out what is known as a 'mass screen' and tested the DNA of 5,000 men who lived in the same locality – none of which matched the semen stains either. And the breakthrough only came when one of the tested men was overheard boasting that he had been paid to masquerade for testing purposes as a local baker called Colin Pitchfork.

In July 1988, after DNA in a sample definitively taken from Pitchfork had provided a match, he was convicted of both murders and sentenced to life in prison. As well as being the first person in the world to be identified as the result of mass DNA screening, Colin Pitchfork was also the first person to be convicted of murder based on DNA evidence.

Sometimes, following the development of new tests and techniques such as DNA profiling, forensic scientists are asked to look again at 'cold cases' involving crimes that occurred many years ago and were never solved. One such case that I worked on originally in 1981, during my years at the FSS, involved the murder of seventeen-year-old Claire Woolterton.

Claire's naked, mutilated body was discovered on a footpath beside the river in Windsor in the early hours of an August morning. No semen was found on any of the swabs taken from her body, and a single, light-brown hair found on her buttocks turned out to be similar in colour and microscopic appearance to her own. Claire was lying on her front when her body was discovered. But I wrote in my original statement (in October 1981) that the heavy bloodstaining on her upper front and back indicated that she had lain on her back at some time after her injuries were inflicted – in other words, that her body had been moved.

It was also my opinion that all the blood on the path could have been the result of passive bleeding from her injuries, and that there was nothing to indicate those injuries had been inflicted there. So it looked as though she had been killed elsewhere before her body was left on the footpath on which she was found.

The police had identified several possible suspects and we examined numerous items from them. These included nail scrapings, blood and saliva samples, a blanket, clothing, boots, knives and other household items, and swabs taken from a car. We also examined numerous knives that had been found at various locations close to and within about a twenty-mile (32-km) radius of the footpath by the river. But test results for all of the items showed no obvious connection with the dead woman, and the trail seemed to go cold.

The case remained unsolved when I was contacted by Thames Valley Police in 2012 and asked to provide information about some samples I had taken during the original investigation. Although more than thirty years had passed by that time, I could remember the case, which had haunted me because of the nature of Claire's death and the fact that the scene had never been identified, so we'd had very little to work on. I could recall taking samples at the time and could see from some photographs that the police sent me, and from a video of the post-mortem examination, that they consisted of tapings taken from various parts of Claire's body.

Tapings are clear strips of sticky tape that are applied sequentially to clothing, parts of the body, the insides of vehicles and other surfaces with which an offender or victim may have had contact during the commission of an offence. As well as textile fibres, tapings will pick up flakes of skin, fragments of dried body-fluid staining, and a wide variety of other loosely adhering small particles and transferred trace materials such as paint flakes, wood fragments, soil and other debris.

In this case, there were further tapings from the low wall at the scene, and a polythene bag containing small stones, gravel and some dried brown leaves and twigs. Fortunately, there were also the notes I had written at the time, as well as my subsequent report. So there were at least *some* items and information that could prove useful in the new investigation.

During the intervening period, the murder had occurred in the Thames Valley area in 1984 of 29-year-old Deirdre Sainsbury. A year later, a travelling salesman called Colin Campbell had been found guilty of her murder and sentenced to life in prison.

Deirdre had been hitchhiking when Campbell picked her up in Roehampton, in south-west London, then strangled her and dumped her mutilated body near a golf course. By the time the investigation into Claire Woolterton's death was re-opened as a cold case, Campbell had successfully appealed to have his conviction for killing Deirdre Sainsbury reduced to manslaughter, on the grounds that the epilepsy from which he suffered had resulted in the attack.

Campbell was not one of the suspects in the original investigation into Claire's death, and for many years he must have thought he had, quite literally, got away with murder. What he perhaps hadn't been aware of, however, were the huge advances that had been made in forensic science in general during those years, and in DNA profiling in particular, or that DNA remains in good condition for many years, and perfectly testable if kept in cool, dry conditions.

So scientists at the FSS looked at some of the adhesive tapings I had taken from Claire's body more than thirty years earlier. When they analysed the DNA on them, they found that it matched Campbell's DNA, with less than a one in a million chance that it could have come from someone else who was unrelated to him.

When questioned, Campbell denied any involvement in Claire's murder. But after a professor of statistics at University

College London analysed the DNA results further and stated that the chance of the DNA not being the suspect's was closer to one in a billion, Campbell was charged with murder.

I gave evidence at the trial about the background to the tapings, to link the old investigation with the new one. And in December 2013, Colin Campbell was found guilty of murdering Claire Woolterton and given a life sentence, to run concurrently with the sentence he was already serving.

Sometimes, the analytical results of DNA samples from unidentified bodies or from items seized in relation to historic crimes are compared with reference samples from specific people in order to check whether they could have been the source. This can also be done on a larger scale to try to identify bodies in mass graves following conflicts and natural disasters.

The reference DNA samples that are used in these cases may be from family members or surrogate samples obtained from items belonging to the missing person(s). Essentially, surrogate samples are taken from items that are likely to contain DNA from the person of interest. These include clothing, toothbrushes and hairbrushes habitually used by that person before their death or seized by police during an original investigation. A good example of the use of surrogate samples was in the case involving the horrific murder on 14 February 1988 of Lynette White.

When Lynette's body was found in a flat above a shop in Cardiff, she had more than fifty stab wounds and her throat and wrists had been slashed. In November 1990, despite the absence of any forensic evidence to connect them with the crime, three of the original five black and mixed-race suspects were found guilty of Lynette's murder and sentenced to life in prison. Two years later, the convictions of the men who had become known as the 'Cardiff Three' were quashed by the Court of Appeal amid concerns that the police had forced confessions out of them.

Another eight years were to pass before the case was re-opened, when new techniques made it possible to detect and examine traces of DNA that had been found at the crime scene. By that time, two of the original five defendants had died. So surrogate samples from items that had been seized from them during the original investigation, and on which they would have been expected to have left their DNA, were used to establish their DNA profiles. But none of the DNA from any of the original suspects matched that found at the crime scene.

Eventually, a familial search of the National DNA Database led to a fourteen-year-old boy whose DNA was on the database because he had been convicted of some minor offence, but who had not yet been born at the time of Lynette's murder. By testing samples that were taken from male family members, a match was found with the boy's uncle, Jeffrey Gafoor. When the case went to court in 2003, Gafoor pleaded guilty to murder and was sentenced to life in prison – and the Cardiff Three were finally and definitively exonerated.

Databases are critical to our ability to identify who might be responsible for a crime when DNA has been left behind at the crime scene or on the victim, for example. They also enable us to assess the strength of the link between a DNA profile and a particular suspect or victim, and give an idea of how frequently each of the DNA components that make up the profile occurs in the population at large. And they allow information to be shared with those in other countries, which helps in the identification and tracking of criminals who may live overseas or be on the run.

The range of investigative tools at the disposal of forensic scientists has been expanded and enriched during recent years by information derived from computers, mobile phones and CCTV. However, DNA profiling remains, without doubt, one of the most powerful weapons in the fight against crime. So it is important to ensure that people – including jurors – are not blinded by the science of statistics. For example, it might sound impressive to be able to say that there is a 1 in 600,000 chance of the DNA profile obtained from a sample of saliva belonging to anyone *other* than the suspect. But with a current UK population of approximately 67 million, what that actually means – in theory, at least – is that there are 110 or more other people in the UK whose DNA it could alternatively be.

One notable case that served as a very important reminder about the care that needs to be taken when assessing the significance of DNA evidence, even when the statistics look pretty good, concerned a man charged with a burglary in Bolton, in the north-west of England, in 2000.

The suspect's DNA profile matched one obtained from a sample taken from the crime scene, which had been estimated to occur in only 1 in 37 million people. On the face of it, the proposition that the man was the source of the DNA must have seemed reasonable – and he wouldn't have been the first – or last – suspect to deny strongly ever having been near the burgled premises. In this case, however, it was a denial that he was able to support with a cast-iron alibi. So the police ordered a re-test of the sample, which was performed using a newly upgraded form of analysis that looked at ten areas of DNA rather than just the original six. And what the new test demonstrated emphatically was that the man could not, after all, be the source of the DNA in question.

In our current DNA profiling technique, in which we look at seventeen areas of DNA (including one that indicates gender), the chance of two unrelated people having the same full profile is less than one in a billion. But where only partial profiles have been achieved, and the statistics are a bit lower, it is necessary to exercise a degree of caution about what you are able to conclude.

In addition to blood and semen stains, nail clippings and scrapings (usually taken with a cocktail stick) are also important samples for forensic scientists when there is any suspicion of a violent struggle between two people. For example, skin (and possibly blood) can be transferred to the victim's nails if they manage to scratch their attacker's face, and DNA profiling can then provide the all-important link with someone in particular.

Of course, if the offender has been identified at an early stage, their face may well show evidence of scratch marks. Or witnesses may describe such marks on the faces of people they know who could conceivably be associated with the attack. Other sorts of evidence, such as tiny fragments of textile fibres from clothing or particles of soil, can also become trapped under nails and provide useful additional links in such cases.

Nails can feature in casework in other ways too. For example, parts of them can be torn off in fights and left behind unnoticed at crime scenes. Longitudinal ridges on the nail, which are produced during normal growth, can also be pattern matched with nail cuttings from a suspect. These days though, scientists are likely to go straight for DNA profiling as a means of linking nail clippings with the person from whom they came.

One case in which nail clippings proved to be critical evidence in an investigation involved a murder that occurred in 2017 in one of the offices of a large international company. By that time, I had co-founded the company Axiom International Ltd, and we were doing increasing numbers of cases overseas.

After the body of an employee of one of the company's subcontractors was found lying in a pool of his own blood in his office, some fifty suspects were taken in for questioning. While some of them were of more interest than others, there seemed to be no evidence to connect any of them with the murder. So the police authorities turned to forensic science.

When our crime scene investigator and forensic biologist inspected the scene, they collected various items and samples. Among the samples, which they brought back to our laboratory in the UK for analysis, were nail scrapings and clippings they had taken from the dead man in the mortuary. When these were subjected to DNA profiling, the results represented a mixture of DNA from the victim and someone else. When the non-victim elements were analysed and compared with reference samples from the suspects, it wasn't long before a match was found.

Faced with the evidence, the suspect confessed to the crime, and also implicated his colleague. According to the suspect, the two men had gone to their boss's office to talk to him about being overworked. Following an altercation, the suspect held the victim's hand while the other man hit him several times with a wooden object.

After both suspects were subsequently arrested, there were reports in the press of the important role forensic science had played in the investigation. And although it hasn't been possible to ascertain whether the case ever went to trial, I have included it here as an example of an investigation in which nail clippings provided decisive DNA evidence in a case that might otherwise have proved very difficult to solve.

Of course, it isn't just forensic scientists and others involved on the investigative side of criminal activity who are aware of the evidential power of DNA. One incident related to someone being suspected of going to extreme lengths to avoid being associated with a crime committed some years earlier. The man had refused to give a DNA sample when he was arrested for another crime. In the event though, his refusal didn't matter, the senior investigating officer explained to him, because the FSS laboratory concerned already had his DNA from another case.

Shortly afterwards, two of my colleagues who were on call for lab security issues were alerted to a fire at the laboratory.

The fire brigade arrived within three minutes of the alarms going off, and my colleagues got there not long afterwards. But despite the prompt response, the damage caused by the fire was extensive. In fact, according to a subsequent parliamentary report, damage to buildings and equipment was finally estimated at £750,000.

Whoever had set fire to the lab and to some key Crown Prosecution Service offices – later alleged to have been two associates paid by the suspect who had refused to give a DNA sample – had drilled holes through the wooden window frames and external doors. They had then used garden Hozelock sprayers to pump in petrol under pressure, followed by a firework to ignite it.

As soon as my colleagues were able to enter the building, they emptied all the freezers – which were only charred on the outside – and took the undamaged contents offsite to other laboratories. Among these undamaged contents were the DNA-refusing suspect's samples.

The fire ended up affecting 168 samples, including those taken from crime scenes and suspects relating to thirty-seven offences, for which all the available forensic evidence was lost. Worryingly, the arsonists seemed to have been aware of the layout of the lab and which part of it to target. And while no one was ever charged with the crime, it certainly caused the FSS to step up its security arrangements.

Current forensic DNA techniques focus on analysing regions of DNA that are highly variable between different people, and therefore enable us to distinguish between them as potential sources of blood or other body-fluid stains. However, the next generation of techniques that are currently being validated for forensic use are much more exciting. This is because they are starting to provide at least some information about what the person from whom the DNA has come might look like in terms of their hair and eye colour, skin tone and propensity to go bald, for example. They also provide a further level of detail that makes it easier to deconvolute the sort of mixed profiles we get at the moment when contributors to the mixture may share some of the same DNA components.

During an interview I did some years ago for a TV or radio programme – I can't remember now which it was – I mentioned that one day we would be able to put a DNA sample from blood or saliva in one end of a machine and get a printed photofit-type picture out at the other end. It was a view that has always been shared by my forensic colleagues, the only debate among us being in relation to the timescale. But another contributor to the interview responded by stating that what I was saying was nonsense. If he's still alive today, he'll presumably see that we're on track to making this possible.

7

Hair

Early on in my forensic career, I was quite surprised by how many murder victims had hairs in or on their hands. Very often, the hairs turned out to be their own, possibly due to them having their hands up over their heads when they were being attacked. But sometimes it was someone else's hair – their assailant's, for example, because they had fought back while they were being attacked.

One case I worked on at the request of the defendant's solicitor involved a woman who had been accused of planting two crudely constructed incendiary devices in a shop in a town on the south coast of England. One of the devices consisted of a carrier bag containing some newspaper wrapped around with Sellotape, together with a plastic sheet, two plastic bags, one of which contained firelighters, and some matches. There were also some hairs and fibres in the carrier bag, which were submitted to the FSS laboratory at Chepstow for comparison with a reference sample of head hair from the suspect, who I'll call Jennifer Bowling.*

The hairs from the device were a tangled mass of mid- to dark-brown head hair, with roots that indicated they had fallen out naturally rather than being pulled out. When examined by a scientist using a comparison microscope, the hairs

* Not her real name.

were found to be microscopically indistinguishable from the suspect's hairs. And when dyestuff from sections of selected hairs was removed and analysed by thin-layer chromatography, it was found to be similar in the two samples – which, the scientist reported, was 'good evidence' of a link with Bowling.

When I visited the FSS laboratory almost a year after the incident, I examined the hair samples and checked the lab records related to the analysis of the dyestuff in them. As a result, I was able to confirm the scientist's findings, insofar as to say that Bowling *could* have been the source of the hairs found on the incendiary device. What lent additional weight to this conclusion was the similarity between the dyestuffs in the two samples.

The question that then had to be addressed was how the hairs came to be associated with the device. After checking the statements of the people who had been involved in seizing the hair exhibit and taking the hair samples from Bowling, I concluded that there had apparently been little opportunity for contamination by the police officers involved. In fact though, this was more or less ruled out by the difference in regrowth after dyeing between the two samples – i.e. the distance of the starting point of dyeing from the root end, indicating hair growth. Therefore, I agreed with the FSS scientist that the hair evidence seemed to be good evidence of a link between the incendiary device and Bowling – which was reflected by the guilty verdict that was delivered in court.

Hair is a useful type of evidence for forensic scientists to look for because we naturally lose, on average, between 70 and 100 hairs a day from our heads. These can then find their way on to the clothing of other people we may come into contact with, into cars we travel in, places we visit and objects we handle. Hairs can also be forcibly removed in cases of assault, when they may be found on weapons and are often associated with blood, skin tissue and other body fluids.

But it isn't only human hairs that interest forensic scientists. Animal-hair identification and comparison are important too, for example in cases involving allegations of bestiality, the theft of high-value fur coats and sheep worrying. They can also provide a means of linking the clothing of one person with another through the hair of domestic pets. Animal hairs can be distinguished from each other and from human hairs mainly by differences in their microscopic appearance, but also by mitochondrial DNA profiling.

Hair is essentially a dead structure, attached to the body by a root that sits inside a sheath of living cells known as a follicle. The structure of a hair can be compared to that of a pencil. It has a central core, known as the medulla (equivalent to the pencil lead), and a surrounding cortex (the wooden part of the pencil), which contains the pigment granules that give the hair its colour. There is also an outer cuticle (the painted outer surface of the pencil) composed of overlapping scales, which protects the hair from the environment.

Hair grows at different rates depending on the part of the body, and also on factors such as age, gender, hair colour and ethnicity. The fastest growing hair is scalp hair, which grows about half an inch (1 cm) a month. Hairs from different parts of the body also look different when viewed under a microscope, so it is possible to distinguish a head hair from an eyebrow hair, or a pubic or body hair, for example. Hairs from the same person's head can also be seen to be different in terms of their colour and internal features when compared to each other, and along the length of each individual strand. The hair types of people from different ethnic groups are also markedly different from each other.

The fact that there can be considerable overlap between hairs from different people in the same case will severely limit what the scientists can say about who they could have come from based on appearance alone. So comparing samples of a suspect's hair with hairs found on a body, clothing or other item from a crime scene rarely provides very strong evidence of a connection, unless it is supported by some other form of evidence.

Sometimes, if the hair is unusual in some respect – perhaps, as in the case above, because it has been bleached, dyed or damaged in some way – it is possible to draw rather firmer conclusions about its potential origin.

A specialised type of DNA profiling called mitochondrial profiling can be performed on lengths of hair shaft, although this is far less discriminating than regular DNA profiling. Of course, if the roots of the hairs have been pulled out, taking some follicle cells with them, these cells can be analysed to provide a standard DNA profile that can then transform a hair link into a very powerful one indeed.

In one case that remained unsolved for fifteen years, it was a single hair on a taping from the victim's neck that helped to identify a killer.

Amy Shepherd – known affectionately as 'the Duchess' – was a sociable, smartly dressed 86-year-old woman living in sheltered accommodation near Halifax when she was subjected to a sustained and brutal attack in her home in August 2004. Strangled with her own tea towel and stabbed in the neck, Amy suffered several fractured ribs and was sexually assaulted. Two rings, a watch and a small amount of cash were later found to be missing.

Numerous items and samples were taken from the scene and the body for examination at the FSS laboratory at Wetherby. But no real evidence was found to link the murder with any of the people of interest who emerged from the police investigation. So the police stored the items and samples in case any new information subsequently came to light or any new scientific techniques were developed that might help to identify who was responsible for Amy's death.

In 2009, the case was reviewed, and among the stored evidential items that were examined were the tea towel, some swabs from intimate parts of Amy's body, and a single hair on a taping from her neck. The hair had a root on it, and when this was subjected to the most sensitive form of DNA profiling available at that time, a partial DNA profile was obtained that seemed to contain a small amount of DNA from Amy mixed with some from someone else. Mixed results were still difficult to interpret, and it was not possible to identify the source of the 'foreign' (i.e. non-Amy) DNA. So the case remained unsolved for another ten years, until the police decided to conduct a second review in 2019.

By then, new, more sensitive DNA profiling techniques had been developed. And when the original extract made from the hair was re-tested by the forensic scientist Ed Jarman, it yielded a full single-source DNA profile. Improvements and advances had also been made in the software used to interpret complex DNA results, and when applied to the 2009 results, these were found to match the new result.

One of the reference samples from the original people of interest was from a man called Raymond Kay. At the time when Amy Shepherd was killed, Kay – who had an extensive criminal record for house burglary, theft and deception – was delivering Meals on Wheels to her as part of a community service sentence. And it was his reference sample that matched the one Ed had obtained from the hair found on Amy's neck.

Ed then tested a high vaginal swab that had been taken by the pathologist at the murder scene, using the Y-STR technique that analyses male-specific DNA. Again, the DNA profile matched Kay. Tests of several areas of the tea towel also revealed two that contained DNA to which Kay could have contributed. And in May 2019, seventy-year-old

Raymond Kay was found guilty of the murder of Amy Shepherd and sentenced to life in prison.

Scientists in North America used to place a lot more emphasis on the microscopic detail of the appearance of hairs and come up with much stronger evidence of association than we have ever done in the UK. But this eventually came back to bite them a few years ago when DNA evidence cast doubt on their conclusions, as a result of which several court verdicts were overturned.

The fact that the hair evidence in so many cases in the US was found to be flawed highlights the variability of hairs and the limitations of hair-by-hair comparisons based on appearance alone. For true strength of evidence, you need to take a holistic view of hair samples and try to obtain some DNA results from them.

8

Cold cases

Whenever you are working on a case, it is always the most important case you've ever done. Sometimes, cases don't go to court for months, even years, after we've worked on them. And some don't ever go to court, perhaps because the forensic investigation has indicated that a particular suspect wasn't involved after all. It's always satisfying to know that you've helped to 'crack' a case, whether that involves linking a suspect with a crime or helping to prove the innocence of a defendant. But, for any forensic scientist, the only thing that really matters is using science to help establish the truth. So it has been particularly satisfying over the years to have helped to solve numerous cold cases and to identify, once and for all, the perpetrators of crimes that had begun to look as though they might never be solved.

By the mid-1990s, Forensic Access had become well established. During the years when I had been working primarily for the defence, my colleagues and I had become increasingly aware of weaknesses in the prosecution's forensic evidence in quite a few cases. And it was that new perspective that led to the setting up, in 1997, of my next company, Forensic Alliance. As well as working on a range of cases for either side – prosecution or defence – the idea behind setting up Forensic Alliance was particularly to give the police a choice of forensic provider so they didn't always have to go to the FSS, and/or could obtain an authoritative second opinion if they wanted one.

Senior officers at several police forces had assured me that they would use our services if we set up the new company. But, suddenly, when Forensic Alliance was up and running, they all became anxious about being criticised as the first to do so. That was when I had the idea of offering to work on a cold case: if we didn't solve it, it wouldn't reflect badly on the particular police force involved, because no one would know we had been working on it; but if we were successful, they would be able to take all the credit.

A cold case is a criminal investigation that remains unsolved, due to lack of evidence, but open. This means that it can be investigated again should new evidence arise, some new scientific technique become available, or a new approach be shown to be successful so that stored evidential items might usefully be re-examined.

Cold cases aren't yesterday's problem. There will always be cases that aren't solved at the time and that become the cold cases of tomorrow. Re-investigations of old – particularly high-profile – cases have always been carried out, usually as the result of new information coming to light. With the introduction of DNA profiling in the mid-1980s, this type of investigation was taken to a whole new level. But it isn't only DNA profiling that has contributed to the dramatic success of cold-case investigations in recent years. And in response to other factors, such as the increased sophistication of other analytical processes, forensic scientists have become increasingly skilled in finding tiny traces to test and in the subtle art of looking for some types of evidence in order to be able to find others.

The first cold case we looked at involved the murder in 1988 of twenty-year-old Lynette White (see Chapter 6). After reviewing the original forensic examination, which had been conducted primarily at the FSS laboratory in Chepstow, we produced an initial report in 1999. A few months later, we were asked to conduct our own re-investigation of the case. Our brief was to try to establish what had actually taken place on the night Lynette was murdered, and who might have been responsible for her death.

It was realised very early on that in the original investigation some 'foreign' blood had been identified at the crime scene – i.e. blood that could not have come from Lynette herself, and that might therefore be the offender's. But the blood-grouping techniques available at the time were simply not sufficiently discriminating to indicate whose blood this might have been.

One of the things that struck me when I read the report of one of the original forensic examinations was the presence of a Y chromosome in samples of blood from Lynette's jeans and sock, which had been attributed to a self-confessed female witness to the attack. But the fact that Y chromosomes are only present in males meant either that the alleged witness's blood must have been mixed with male blood, or that it couldn't have been her blood at all.

By the time we became involved in the case, DNA profiling had been introduced, and some advances had been made in the techniques that were used. So we were able to show that the blood from the jeans and sock and from other samples that we extracted from items stored by the FSS and police was a familial match for a fourteen-year-old boy whose DNA profile was on the national database and whose uncle, Jeffrey Gafoor, eventually admitted to killing Lynette White and was subsequently tried and convicted.

In view of the highly sophisticated DNA-profiling techniques that have been developed over the last thirty years, it may surprise some people to learn that dust and fluff are still two of the forensic scientist's most valued 'informants'. In addition to tapings, scientists may use shaking to dislodge particles from the surfaces of items in the laboratory. Brushing with a disposable toothbrush is the method often employed to recover tiny particulate traces from inside pockets, the seams of clothing, and even the inner seams of exhibit bags where debris that has fallen off the evidential item itself is likely to have gathered. This last approach was used to great effect when we became involved in the cold-case investigation into the murder of nineteen-year-old Black student Stephen Lawrence.

Stephen had been waiting with a friend for a bus on a street in south-east London on the evening of 22 April 1993 when he was attacked and stabbed by a group of white youths. Despite tip-offs from people who claimed to be able to identify Stephen's killers, it was two weeks before the police made any arrests. But all five suspects were subsequently released without charge.

I first became involved in the case two years later, when Stephen's family were preparing to take out a private prosecution. After spending a week at the Metropolitan Police Forensic Science Laboratory in London checking the work that had been done by the scientists there, and then doing some further investigations myself, I wrote a report for the Lawrence family. In that report, I concluded that the lack of any scientific evidence to connect the defendants with Stephen was unsurprising, in view of the amount of time that had elapsed before they were arrested.

Unfortunately, the private prosecution collapsed when the young man who was with Stephen at the time of the attack – and had run off expecting Stephen to follow him, before going back to try to help his friend – was found to be an unreliable witness.

I didn't give evidence at that hearing. But I did do so to the inquiry that was commissioned by the Home Secretary in 1997, when I said that I agreed with the FSS scientists' conclusions that there was only weak evidence connecting any of the suspects' clothing with Stephen. I did add, however, that this lack of evidence could not be used as a point in support of the defence, because in the specific circumstances, not much evidence would have been expected to be transferred.

The resulting Macpherson Report, which was published in 1999, raised issues of institutional racism in the Metropolitan Police Service. One of the recommendations made in the report was that the law of double jeopardy – which prevented someone being tried again for a crime for which they had already been acquitted – should be repealed. The change came into effect in England and Wales in 2005, and a year later I was approached again about the Stephen Lawrence case, by which time I was working with the company LGC Forensics.

After an initial interest in paint, we had been focusing on a search for textile fibres that could have been transferred between the clothing Stephen had been wearing and that belonging to the original murder suspects. After having some success, we extended our search to the original packaging of some items, when forensic examiner April Robson was surprised to discover a tiny flake of blood in the exhibit bag in which the jacket of one of the suspects had been stored. There had been other searches for blood on the suspects' clothing – including some we had done ourselves, with no success – but no one had previously thought to examine the packaging.

When the flake of blood was examined, it was found to contain DNA that matched Stephen's. Then two blue textile fibres that had become encased within the flake when the blood was wet were shown to match textile fibres from the cardigan Stephen had been wearing at the time he was killed, which strengthened the other fibre evidence that we had already discovered. As well as representing the 'golden nugget' of scientific evidence that finally helped to solve the case, the discoveries were also good examples of the invaluable role something as apparently inconsequential as dust and fluff can play in even the most complex of criminal investigations.

In the forensic investigation into the Pembrokeshire Coastal Path murders, it was sweepings from the floor of suspect John Cooper's shed that contained some vital evidence. In this case, textile fibres that were found in the sweepings linked Cooper to items of clothing he had abandoned in hedgerows after committing burglaries in the local area, and which, in turn, could be linked to several of his victims.

Following the murders in June 1989 of a couple on the Pembrokeshire Coastal Path in Wales, the search for additional textile fibres led to another discovery. This time, it was a tiny spot of victim Peter Dixon's blood on the suspect's shorts. This was followed by what appeared at first to be the impossible-to-explain discovery inside the upturned hem of the shorts of DNA that matched that of the murdered couple's daughter. But when the pieces of the jigsaw were fitted together, it helped lead to the conviction in 2011 of serial killer John Cooper for four murders, a rape and serious sexual assault. It also served as another important example of truth often being 'stranger than fiction' in real-life forensics.

It was noticing that there was something odd about the original analytical results that helped to unlock another cold case. Rachel Nickell was just twenty-three years old when she was murdered in a horrific knife attack while walking with her young son on Wimbledon Common in south-west London on 15 July 1992. The case wasn't solved at the time, and we became involved in the cold-case investigation some ten years later.

The attack on Rachel appeared to have been sexually motivated. So scientists at the MPFSL examined tapings taken from parts of her body that had been exposed when her lower clothing was pulled down, in the hope of finding some male DNA that could have come from her killer.

The problem was, not only did they not find any of the male DNA they were looking for, but they didn't find any DNA at all. This should have been an indication that something was wrong, as the tape should at least have been covered with Rachel's own skin cells and DNA.

This time it was by noticing and correcting what turned out to be a flaw in the original scientists' technique on this critical sample that we uncovered traces of DNA matching that of serial rapist and murderer Robert Napper. We then found paint and footwear-mark links to him. And when Napper was convicted of Rachel Nickell's murder in 2008, long-term suspect Colin Stagg was finally exonerated. Correcting the technical flaw also ensured that a number of other 'dormant' cases could be solved.

Another case that remained unsolved for a few years involved the death in November 2000 of ten-year-old Damilola Taylor, who bled to death in the stairwell of a block of flats in south-east London after the artery in his thigh was severed with a shard of glass.

We were asked to look at the case just over four years later. And it was simply by conducting a more thorough search of clothing items seized from all of the police's original suspects that we found some of Damilola's blood on items belonging to suspects Danny and Ricky Preddie, who had been apprehended just five days after the killing. Four young people had already been tried for the crime, two of whom were acquitted when the case collapsed, while the other two had been found not guilty. So, again, the evidence we discovered finally put paid to any suggestion that any of them had anything to do with Damilola's death.

One of the early cold cases I investigated was the death in 1982 of Italian banker Roberto Calvi, who was found hanging from some scaffolding that had been erected underneath Blackfriars Bridge in London.

The case was to prove transformational in my growth as a forensic scientist as it demonstrated how ten years later, and with very few items to examine – just the outer clothing Calvi was wearing at the time, the stones with which his body had been weighted, and the rope from around his neck – it was possible to provide convincing answers to central questions such as 'Did he commit suicide or was he murdered?' In this case, it seemed that Calvi had definitely been murdered (see Chapter 17), and this was accepted by the Italian courts, who went on to charge and attempt to prosecute a number of suspects.

There are many additional challenges with cold-case investigations. These include the fact that the crime scene in its original state is long gone, so you have to rely on plans and photographs, police briefings, witness descriptions, and initial forensic and other expert reports and case notes to recreate it in the mind's eye. In addition, it may be very difficult to locate some of the key items after the passage of time, and most, if not all, of them will already have been examined and the best samples taken for testing. Also, and critically, this examination and testing may have been carried out in conditions that were not as well controlled and stringent as they have to be today. This can create opportunities for accidental contamination, which also tends to be magnified because of the much more complicated history of the items involved.

One example of this type of complicating factor is the number of times an item may have been taken in and out of its bag and re-examined. This may have occurred over quite an extended period of time, and in different locations by different people. In these circumstances, it is critical to consider all aspects of the handling and storage of the item, and to assess whether anything related to these could conceivably provide an alternative, innocent explanation for the apparent evidence.

But nothing beats the satisfaction of overcoming these sorts of additional challenges and being able to contribute to evidence that either helps to convict the guilty or to exonerate the innocent – or both – and to know that our communities are slightly safer and fairer as a consequence.

I wrote at the start of this chapter that at the time of working on a case it is the most important one you've ever done. The reason why it's useful to feel like this is because, especially with the larger cases, it means that you automatically pull out *all* the stops. You have to be at your most imaginative, so that you can find ways into the evidence; particularly tenacious, so that you go on looking for long enough; especially meticulous, so that you don't miss anything; even more collaborative than usual, so that you surround yourself with people who have all the knowledge and skills you might conceivably need; and very communicative, so that you take investigators with you and they don't cut off funding for the work too soon.

Every case is different, which means that you are constantly learning how to improve your chances of success. And it was developing a better understanding of forensic science and passing on critical lessons learned that were two of the main reasons why I decided to start writing about forensics in the way that I have.

9

The importance of independent checks

It was the early hours of the morning of 28 January 2006 and Detective Inspector Michael Ornellas had been asleep in bed when he was awoken by a loud crashing sound. Running out on to the landing, he saw that the lower part of the staircase was on fire. Fortunately, he managed to get his wife and three sons to safety.

A few minutes later, Detective Sergeant Martin Brough was also at home with his family when he heard loud banging noises coming from the front of the house. On going to investigate, he discovered that the front door and an adjacent panel were on fire. Fortunately again, he and his family also escaped unhurt.

In both cases, the fire brigade was called and the fires were extinguished.

There were broken milk bottles and a smell of petrol at both locations, and a number of items were taken from the properties for closer inspection, including two black beanie hats from the first fire scene, and lumps of concrete from both of them. When these were examined by scientists at the FSS laboratory at Huntingdon, tufts of grey nylon microfibres were discovered on two lumps of concrete taken from the first address as well as on the two hats – from inside one of which it proved possible to obtain a mixed DNA profile of the wearers.

Three suspects emerged during the police investigation: Angelo DeBono, Jason Eagles and someone I'll call Defendant C. No potential sources for the grey microfibres were identified among any items that had been seized from them. But the DNA in the hat could have represented a mixture of DNA from DeBono and Defendant C. Partly on the basis of this evidence, all three suspects were charged with attempted murder and arson with intent to endanger life.

We were instructed by solicitors acting for Defendant C, who denied any knowledge of the offences and said he had never seen the concrete before. He did admit to having had a black beanie hat, however, which he said he had last seen about a month before the incidents, when he had left it hanging up with his overalls at the garage belonging to his girlfriend's father, where he had been working. Apparently, Jason Eagles also had a job in a garage and would often visit the one in which Defendant C worked, so would have had access to the hat there.

When we examined the hats and lumps of concrete, we were able to confirm that all the grey microfibres recovered from them matched each other, and therefore could have come from the same source, although it wasn't clear what that source might have been. Certainly, there was nothing to suggest it could have been Defendant C, as a search of his car and home address failed to reveal any similar fibres.

We then considered the possibility that some of the fibres might have arisen through some sort of contamination, either at the scene or afterwards. As well as taking account of factors such as how common fibres of that type were, we thought about the mechanism by which they might have been transferred on to the items on which they were found at the crime scene. We also inspected the DNA results in relation to the hat and confirmed that Defendant C's DNA could have contributed to it, as claimed by the prosecution.

All in all, it looked as though the black beanie hat with the DNA in it probably did belong to Defendant C. But there was no evidence to suggest that he had worn it on the night in question, or that he could have been the source of the grey microfibres found on it and on the two lumps of concrete. In the context of the case, it was therefore our view that the scientific findings were insufficient to incriminate him in any way. Clearly, the court agreed, as Defendant C was found not guilty on all counts, while DeBono and Eagles were found guilty of arson with intent to endanger life.

Passing sentence, the judge said that he had no doubt the fires had been revenge attacks against the two police officers, who had taken part in a previous operation involving raids on the homes of suspected drug dealers. And because he believed that there was a significant risk of the men committing further offences and causing serious harm, he gave them indeterminate sentences, which would enable them to be kept in jail for longer than determinate sentences would allow.

Two years later, Eagles was re-sentenced and released from prison after providing information that helped in the conviction of a suspected drug dealer, who had apparently organised the two arson attacks and who was sentenced to eighteen years in prison.

There is a principle that 'absence of evidence is not evidence of absence'. But sometimes it comes pretty close. What it means in practical terms is that where there is no, or very little, scientific evidence to link a suspect with a crime, it is always a good idea to explore why this might be. This is particularly important if the prosecution is going to press ahead with the case on other grounds. Even where there *is* an apparent link, however, it may turn out to be meaningless in the context of the specific circumstances of a case – as it did in the case described above.

A very different example of a case in which absence of evidence was certainly a key plank of the defence concerned someone who was charged in connection with the death of a man whose body was found in a culvert.

The suggestion by the prosecution was that, after having a fight with the man, the defendant had dragged him into his house, where he had died during the course of the night. It was claimed that the defendant then borrowed a friend's car, which he used to transport the body to the culvert where it was later found.

No fewer than nine scientists were deployed on the case, variously looking for any evidence in the way of blood, vomit staining, textile fibres, fingerprints, vegetation, drugs and alcohol to support the prosecution's suspicions. The only thing they found were some chemical similarities between some vomit staining outside the defendant's flat and some on the front of the dead man's jacket.

A brief visit a colleague and I made on behalf of the defence to the scene of the alleged crime, and inspection of some of the dead man's clothes, quickly revealed that some evidence should have been found if the defendant was guilty as charged. This included the powdery white substance that had leached out of the concrete walls and ceiling of the culvert and coated everything that came into contact with it, including our own clothing.

There were also several other pieces of evidence that hadn't been mentioned at all. These included damage to the knees of the dead man's jeans and the elbows of his jacket – some of which corresponded with bruises on his body – and minor injuries to his face, as well as to his hands and forearms.

When combined with the fact that the dead man's jacket had been found 100 yards (91 m) upstream – to where it could not possibly have floated – and the very high levels of alcohol in his system, the more likely explanation was that he had fallen into the culvert in a drunken state. Then he had made his own way to where he was found by crawling along the culvert, discarding his jacket on the way and bumping into the culvert wall before he finally passed out and died a few yards further on. This version was accepted by the court, which ruled that the defendant had no case to answer and promptly acquitted him.

It's all too easy to say, 'Oh well, we didn't find any evidence of this specific type because of that particular feature of the case.' But the more times you have to say that, the more concerned you should be that your original hypothesis about the case may be wrong.

Another case involving insufficient evidence was the murder of the well-known journalist and TV presenter Jill Dando.

It was 11.30 a.m. on 26 April 1999 and Jill was about to unlock the front door of her house in Fulham, in south-west London, when she was forced to the ground and shot once in the head. Some of her neighbours apparently saw a man walking away from the house, but didn't realise the potential significance until Jill's body was discovered a few minutes after the shooting.

The extensive police operation that followed involved a team of up to fifty officers. Among the various theories about who had been responsible for Jill's murder was that it was a hit-man hired by an ex-lover; the Serbian authorities, annoyed by an appeal Jill had made on behalf of Kosovo refugees from the war that was taking place at the time; a criminal with a grudge because of her work on the TV programme *Crimewatch*; and an obsessed fan. A year later, a new suspect emerged.

Several years earlier, Barry George had been convicted of attempted rape. According to witnesses – who included his GP – he had been agitated on the day Jill was killed. Two days after Jill's death, in order to prove that he had an alibi, Barry George apparently asked people to verify his movements on that particular day. But in May 2000, he was arrested and charged with murder.

The prosecution's case against the defendant had just four strands: he looked like the man the neighbours saw near the murder scene; he told lies repeatedly during his police interview; he tried to create a false alibi; and a single particle of firearms discharge residue (FDR) that matched other particles at the scene had been found in the pocket of his overcoat.

During the trial, the court heard evidence from three scientists in relation to the FDR particle – which measured the equivalent of 0.01 mm and was found a year after Jill Dando's murder. The two prosecution scientists agreed that the finding was consistent with it having come from the cartridge used in the killing. However, the scientist for the defence maintained that police handling procedures were so poor that it could have arisen from contamination and should not be regarded as evidence. The court concluded that the FDR evidence *was* capable of supporting the prosecution's case, and left it to the jury to decide what weight to assign to it. And in July 2001, Barry George was found guilty of murder and sentenced to life in prison.

In 2007, following an investigation by the Criminal Cases Review Commission and on the basis of new evidence, the case was referred to the Court of Appeal. The new evidence related to developments in interpreting forensic evidence that had been led by the chief statistician of the FSS, Dr Ian Evett. These involved the Case Interpretation and Assessment technique, which Ian and his colleagues had developed. This required forensic scientists to consider the significance of their evidence in terms of the respective support it provided for two competing propositions – one for the prosecution and the other for the defence. In this case, the propositions were that Barry George *was* the man who shot Jill Dando, against the proposition that he *was not* the man who shot her.

Viewed in this way, it became clear that the evidence related to the FDR particle was neutral, because it was as likely to have come from an extraneous source as it was to have come specifically from the gun that killed Jill Dando. In the light of the new guidance, the original prosecution scientists also agreed with this conclusion.

In November 2007, the Court of Appeal quashed Barry George's conviction and ordered a retrial. And in August 2008, after spending eight years in prison, he was finally acquitted of murdering Jill Dando – whose killer is yet to be identified.

Also of critical importance in many cases is that scientific findings are interpreted in the context of all the circumstances of the case, not just some of them. One of the main ways of achieving this is through a second opinion on behalf of the defence.

An example of a case in which a second opinion made all the difference between someone being jailed for life and being able to walk free because the evidence was not capable of proving the case against them involved the death of 51-year-old wife and mother Ana Rebelo.

On 4 April 2017, Ana's fully clothed body was found in her daughter's bed in the flat in Jersey where she lived with her husband and two of their three children. Paramedics who attended the scene found blood coming from her mouth, and she had some minor injuries, including cuts to her lip.

When Ana's husband, Alfredo, was charged with her murder, the forensic evidence against him consisted of DNA, some textile fibres, and damage to the leggings that he said he had removed from around her neck when he found her, but which the prosecution claimed he had used to strangle her.

What was alleged by the prosecution was that on the evening before Ana's body was found, she and Alfredo had an argument, which resulted in him hitting her and causing the injuries to her face. After refusing to sleep with her husband in the master bedroom, Ana had then got into their daughter's bed, which is where she was when Alfredo strangled her with a pair of the daughter's leggings.

A review carried out by some of my colleagues and led by forensic biologist Caroline Crawford suggested that the scientific findings were actually neutral. The basis for this conclusion was that all the evidence could alternatively be explained by the fact that Alfredo lived at the premises and had simply acted in the way he claimed to have done on discovering his wife's body.

The reports we provided prior to Rebelo's trial in January 2019 stated that the evidence related to the damage, DNA and fibres found on the leggings did not help to address the issue of whether any of the three family members present in the house was involved in Ana's death. This coincided with the conclusion reached by the original prosecution forensic scientist. But then another scientist for the prosecution rewrote the entire report. And despite the fact that there were no defensive wounds on Ana Rebelo's body, no signs of any injuries on her husband, and no evidence of a struggle, the second scientist seemed to suggest – without actually saying so explicitly – that, in some respects at least, there *was* evidence of an assault.

The cause of death had been established as compression of the neck, which means lack of blood flow rather than lack of air, and which would have resulted in Ana losing conscious-ness within about ten seconds. So the case for the prosecution rested on the claim that she would therefore only have been able to strangle *herself* if the leggings had been knotted, and had therefore retained the pressure on her neck after she passed out. But this was not the case when the leggings were found next to her body.

What the prosecution overlooked, however, was the fact that the defendant had already said he couldn't remember how the leggings were tied when he removed them from around his wife's neck. And as examination of the damage to them didn't provide any information with respect to the presence or absence of a knot, there really was no evidence either way.

A post-mortem examination had been performed by the pathologist Dr Richard Shepherd, who illustrated the point at the trial by wrapping the leggings around his own leg several times. The fact that they stayed in place sufficiently to cut off the blood flow rendered the knotted-or-not-knotted argument irrelevant anyway. What Dr Shepherd also said was that, although rare, there are numerous documented examples of self-strangulation. When this was added to the other circumstantial evidence that was cast into doubt by the defence, it was enough to highlight the cracks in the prosecution's case. And when the jury returned their verdict, they found Alfredo Rebelo not guilty of murdering his wife.

When a solicitor acting for a defendant asks us to look at the forensic evidence in a case, and at the forensic report written for the prosecution, there are various things they are probably hoping we will find. There may be something wrong with it, for example, or something that hasn't been recognised as being significant, or has even been deliberately glossed over, perhaps through lack of contextual knowledge. Although we often don't find any of these things, sometimes we do, which is why second-opinion work is so critical.

If we do find something, it may be because the police scientist simply wasn't aware of all the circumstances of the case as they emerged during the investigation. This may be because their work will have taken place nearer the beginning than the end of the process. Or there may have been a disconnect between the respective parts of the work that the scientists and their police colleagues have done. Also, there could have been some misunderstanding about what the evidence amounts to because of the brevity with which it has been reported.

Whatever the reason, and especially where forensic science evidence plays a significant part in the case against someone, it is essential that it is properly checked by an appropriately qualified, independent forensic scientist.

10

Crimes against children

However long you've been doing the job, you never get used to crime scenes involving children. They are always deeply unpopular on on-call rotas. But you just have to learn to take a deep breath and try not to think about the child who once wore the bloodstained Babygro that is stretched out in front of you on the laboratory bench. Then, depending on whether you've been instructed by the police or the defence, you do what you would do in any other type of case and focus either on helping to find the person responsible, or on making sure that the scientific evidence is sound and means what it is claimed to mean.

One case I still remember from the time in the late 1970s when I was learning how to conduct forensic crime scene investigations involved the deaths of two young children and their mother. The call to attend came during a bleak winter's afternoon, and it was dark by the time we arrived at the scene, having driven up from the FSS laboratory at Wetherby in West Yorkshire. It had been snowing, and I remember that we were intrigued by some footwear marks in snow outside the house, and that scenes of crime officers were desperately trying to capture images of them in case the snow melted.

The Gibson family's house in Alnwick, in Northumberland, had been set on fire following the killings and the fire damage was extensive. There was no electricity inside the house, so we had to make do with our scene lamps – which were little more than torches, albeit powerful ones – and the light from a large, van-mounted arc light that was shining in through the windows at the front of the house. There was no heating in the house either, and we became increasingly cold as we worked through the early part of the night trying to get an idea of the layout, where the fire had started, and what the cause was likely to have been.

It was the first time I had seen for myself the damage fire can create, and I remember looking at the part-melted remains of a clock that was hanging, Dali-like, on the kitchen wall and making a note of the time on it, because it might have stopped at the point when the heat of the fire reached a certain intensity.

The bodies of the two children had already been removed to the mortuary by the time we arrived, but it was difficult to shake off the feeling that they were still there. What helped was the sense of grim determination that descended on me to use all the scientific skills and knowledge I had acquired to try to discover precisely what had happened to them and who might have been responsible for their violent deaths. I had the same feeling at every crime scene I ever attended, and I have reason to be very grateful for it. Not only did it save me from dwelling too much on the immediate awfulness of what lay in front of me, it also helped me to do my job as well as I possibly could.

On that occasion, as it eventually became obvious that we might do more harm than good in the half-light of the crime scene, we went home to get a few hours' rest before returning to complete the work in daylight.

The following morning, we continued to sift through the ashes and other debris left by the fire, which had caused the upper floor of the house to collapse on to the lower. It was a painstaking process. But it can sometimes yield critical

Sampling bloodstains for DNA profiling at a crime scene.

A complex pattern of blood staining at a crime scene containing a variety of different elements that can be individually identified and used to determine what happened there.

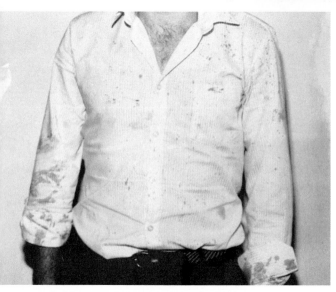

Bloodstain pattern on the shirt of a man who went to the aid of the victim of an assault, showing how much blood can be transferred in these circumstances.

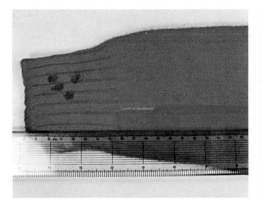

Blood spots on the sleeve of a jumper (left) and after treatment with luminol (right), when tiny traces of blood not visible to the naked eye become apparent, including blood dust from the spots themselves.

A wall at a crime scene (left), and after spraying with luminol (right), highlighting the presence of blood underneath the wallpaper.

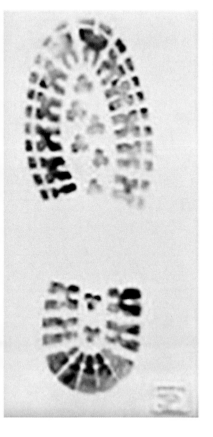

A reference print made from the sole of a suspect's shoe (left) for detailed comparison with a footwear mark left behind on a piece of paper at the crime scene (right).

Tread pattern of the suspect's shoes in a burglary case and in close-up (below).

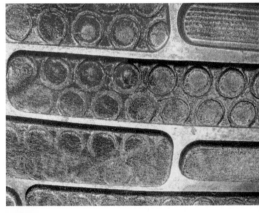

Partial footwear marks deposited on glass at the scene (left), with comparison between a reference mark from the tread pattern of a shoe and marks on the glass (top and bottom, respectively, on the right). This showed that that particular shoe had left the marks on the glass.

Mud staining and abrasion damage to the knees and elbows of the culvert victim's clothing (in the case described in Chapter 9), which helped to show that his death had been accidental and not the result of murder.

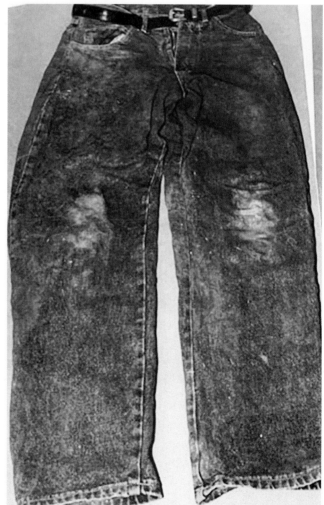

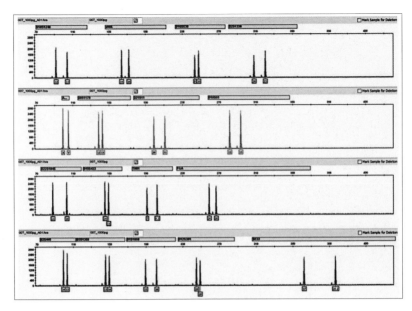

A DNA-profiling result, with each peak on the chart representing a specific component of the DNA within the overall profile.

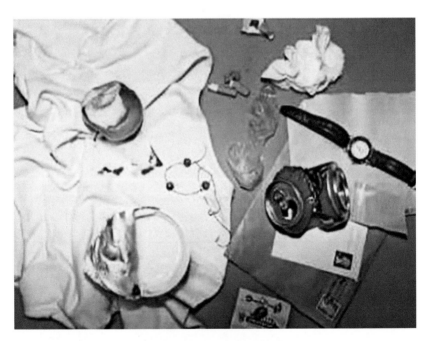

Common examples of items on which DNA from the person who used/wore/ate or drank them can be left behind, and then picked up and profiled by forensic scientists depending on the circumstances.

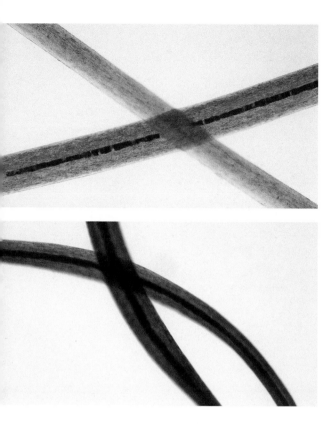

The internal structure of human hair as revealed under the microscope.

One of several hair extensions torn from the victim's head in an assault case, which provided good evidence of a link with the suspect.

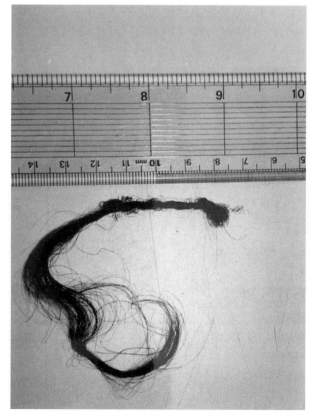

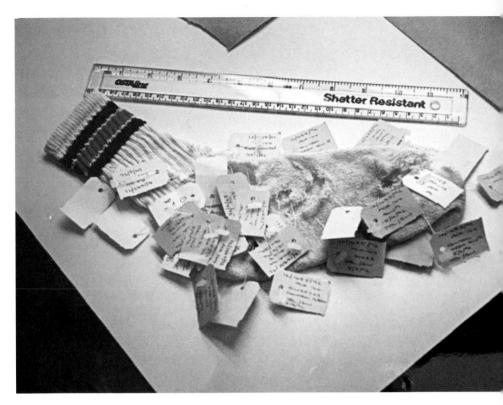

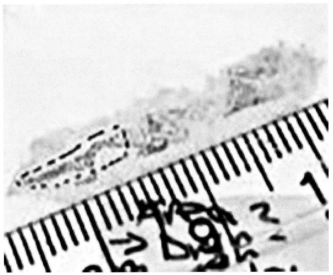

The challenges faced when examining the Lynette White case some years after her murder (Chapter 8) included the fact that there was very little of the potential offender's blood left on her clothing, e.g. her right sock (top). However, scraping the paint off woodwork at the crime scene revealed blood from him that had been deposited at the time of her death (bottom).

evidence – as it did on that occasion, when a gold watchstrap was discovered and identified as belonging to a man called Terence Emery.

Apparently, Emery had been doing building work with the children's father at nearby RAF Boulmer when Mr Gibson reported him for stealing a side of beef. So it was by way of revenge for being sacked that he had killed Eileen Gibson and their children, Andrew, aged three, and Sally, who was six months old.

In October 1979, Terence Emery was found guilty of the murders of Eileen, Sally and Andrew Gibson, and sentenced to eighteen years in prison.

In another very sad case, which I was asked to review for a solicitor, the man he was defending had been accused of being wholly or partly responsible for the assault and subsequent death of his own young child. The main question that needed to be answered was whether the little boy had been assaulted by his father, his mother, or both parents.

When I visited the FSS laboratory where the work had been done, I discussed the forensic scientist's findings with him in detail before examining some of the evidential items and laboratory records myself. Two pathologists who had carried out post-mortem examinations agreed that the child had been subjected to several violent blows to the head and abdomen, which might have included punches to the front of his head and chest. They also said that his head had been banged against some firm and unyielding surface, and his abdomen had been stamped on.

The first thing I needed to consider was the sort of blood-staining you would expect to find with each of the types of assault listed by the pathologists. Successive blows from punching into an area of the child's body that was already wet with blood would have resulted in fine sprays of blood, which would have landed on nearby surfaces, including, especially, the sleeves and front of the assailant's clothing. Banging the little boy's head against an unyielding surface might have resulted in smeared blood, including the characteristic pattern left by wet bloodstained hair, plus spots or splashes cast off from any wounds. Depending on the extent of wet blood-staining on his abdomen, there might also have been a pattern of smeared bloodstains and possibly bloody footwear marks at the point of impact there.

The bloodstaining at the scene had apparently been confined to an area on the bedroom wall about one or two feet (30–60 cm) above the child's cot, where it comprised numer-ous small spots and splashes. The location of the bloodstains and the direction in which some of the droplets had obviously travelled suggested that he might have been struck repeatedly on the head while standing in his cot. But the scientist who had conducted the original forensic investigation had seen nothing to suggest that the child's head had been banged against the wall above his cot. There were no marks on the wallpaper, for example, and no smears of blood that might have indicated an impact site; and no blood was found on the cot, or on the bedding that had been inside it.

Using the phosphoglucomutase (PGM) blood-grouping system – which was one of the most commonly used at that time (in the 1980s) – the forensic scientist had been able to show that while both parents belonged to the same blood group, their child had a different variant of the PGM enzyme. That made it possible to say that blood found on the shirt, trousers and a sock the father had apparently been wearing at the time of the incident had definitely not come from him or his girlfriend, but could have come from their child.

Approximately 40 per cent of the British population have the same PGM blood group as that of the blood found on the items of clothing. So it wasn't proof that it had come from the child, although, with no one else apparently involved, it seemed very likely that it had. But that was for the court to decide.

Some bloodstains on the shoulder and collar of the jumper the mother had been wearing and some watery bloodstains on the father's shirt could have resulted from each of them holding the child against their shoulder after he had sustained the injuries to his head and was bleeding. However, the numerous small spots of blood on the front and right sleeve of the father's shirt could not have come from mere physical contact. The fact that they were typical of the stains produced during a sustained assault, as well as their very small size – 1–3 mm – indicated that the father had been standing close to their source when they were produced.

So, on that occasion, I could only agree with the FSS scientist's conclusion that the bloodstaining at the scene of this tragic crime was consistent with the little boy having been struck on the head while standing in his cot. Although the pattern of blood on the father's shirt fell short of indicating that he *must* have been responsible for his son's injuries, the absence of any similar blood spotting on the mother's clothes tended to strengthen the prosecution's contention that he was. And, apparently, the jury agreed.

What has become apparent recently in relation to crimes against children, particularly, is that there is a link between the abuse of animals and humans. In fact, there are anecdotal reports of animal abuse by numerous notorious killers, including Moors murderer Ian Brady, serial killer Fred West, Steven Barker, who was convicted of causing the death of 'Baby P' and of raping a two-year-old girl, and Aaron Campbell, who, at the age of sixteen, abducted a six-year-old girl from her bed before raping and murdering her.

As recently reported by veterinary surgeon David Martin, in 75 per cent of violent households that have a pet within them, the animal has either been harmed or threatened with harm. This percentage rises even higher, apparently, where there is physical or sexual abuse of a child. The following is just one example of a case with which David and the charity The Links Group have been involved.

In February 2008, an RSPCA inspector paid a visit to a house in Doncaster, where he found a dog in a very sorry state. Limping, and with one bruised and bloodshot eye, the little terrier-cross had apparently been 'disciplined' earlier that day by its male owner, Craig Goddard, for chewing up a maternity hospital bag belonging to his heavily pregnant partner, Lindsay Harris.

According to Harris, she had seen the dog fall down the stairs and crash into the radiator at the bottom after it was hit on the nose by Goddard. But Goddard himself claimed not to have witnessed the fall, and only to have heard the bang, followed by the puppy yelping.

In his report of his visit, the RSPCA inspector noted that the male defendant was pacing anxiously and appeared to be paranoid and upset. So he suspended the interview, and returned a week later to speak to Goddard. Not long after that second visit, Lindsay Harris gave birth to a baby boy; and shortly after that, the couple agreed to the dog being placed in the care of the RSPCA.

Tragically, when little Alfie Goddard was just eleven weeks old, he was admitted to hospital with broken bones and serious head injuries – the result, according to his mother, of him having accidentally fallen down the stairs. It was a story Lindsay Harris stuck to even after Alfie died and her partner was charged with murdering him by squeezing, shaking and dropping him intentionally on the floor in a fit of anger, apparently when the baby was suffering from a stomach ache and couldn't settle.

At his trial in January 2009, Craig Goddard was found guilty of murder and sentenced to life in prison. After eventually pleading guilty to perverting the course of justice, Lindsay Harris was given a suspended prison sentence and ordered to do 150 hours of community service.

During the trial, Goddard's barrister made the comment that, 'This is not a tragedy that could have been anticipated.' But when the evidence related to the *dog's* injuries was subsequently reviewed in the light of Alfie's fate, David Martin – who was the expert witness in the case – concluded in his report that the injuries sustained by the puppy had not been accidental. And what that effectively meant was that Alfie was always likely to be at risk.

Examining the aftermath of any violent assault is always difficult, but even more so when it has involved a child. This is partly because it is overlaid by a sense of the complete betrayal the child may have felt at being abused by an adult whose role – if any – should have been protective. Another aspect is that a young life has been cut short or, at the very least, blighted for ever. Of course, you can't switch off all your emotions just because you're a scientist. But you can divert your energies into trying to find out – as soon as you can, to avoid the same thing happening again – what happened and who might have been responsible.

Water

One afternoon in July 1996, John Copik and his son were trawling off the Devon coast, about six miles (10 km) from Teignmouth, when they hauled in their net and found that it contained the fully clothed body of a man. From its position in the net, John Copik thought the body must have been on the seabed, and that it had been picked up somewhere near Teignmouth. Also in the net, but separate from the body, was a 10-lb (4.5-kg) anchor, which was in good condition and with little or no marine growth on it, suggesting that it had not been in the sea for long.

There was nothing on the body to identify the deceased man. But, thanks to Rolex's meticulous record keeping, he was identified a few weeks later by the 25-year-old Rolex Oyster watch that was still attached to his wrist as a 51-year-old former soldier called Ronald Platt. This was subsequently confirmed by dental records.

Police enquiries led to a friend of Platt's called Albert Walker, who was arrested three months later. Walker owned a yacht called *Lady Jane*, and not long before Platt's body was discovered, he had apparently purchased various items from a shop in Dartmouth that included a 10-lb anchor, which wasn't found when his yacht was searched.

After Walker's arrest, the anchor from the fishing net and a similar one purchased from the same shop for purposes of comparison, as well as various items of clothing from the dead man, were examined at the FSS laboratory in Chepstow. What the scientists there found was that the two anchors were identical and appeared to bear the same label. Also, brown deposits on the shank of the anchor that had been found with the body in the net were microscopically similar to reference samples taken from the leather belt attached through belt hooks to Platt's trousers.

The anchors had a galvanised (zinc) finish, which, on the one that had been caught in the net, had taken on a dull, mottled appearance with areas of whitish corrosion that was consistent with immersion in sea water. The leather belt had a kink in it about ten inches (25 cm) from the buckle, adjacent to which were a number of marks and deposits of translucent material that were found to contain zinc. Together with the marks on the inner, distorted surface of the belt, these could be explained by prolonged contact under wet or damp conditions with an object containing zinc – such as, although not necessarily, the surface of the anchor.

Evidence from two pathologists indicated that the cause of Platt's death was drowning, and that his body had been in water for a week or two at most before it was discovered. One of the pathologists noted three injuries on the body: lacerations on the back of the skull, bruising on the left hip, and fainter bruising lower down on the left leg above the knee. The fact that all of the injuries had occurred before or soon after death ruled out any possibility that they were connected with the act of recovery of the body. It was also the pathologist's view that the injury to the skull could have been caused by a blow to the head that might have resulted in loss of consciousness. And the marks on the leg were consistent with contact with a heavy object, such as an anchor attached to the body by a belt or trouser waistband.

As there were no marks on the body consistent with a violent struggle, another possibility was that the deceased man had placed the anchor in his belt and then entered the water voluntarily. But putting the scientific and medical findings together, and after conducting tests involving inserting the anchor between the belt and trousers, the evidence seemed to support the allegation that it had been attached to Platt by someone else.

What other investigations also revealed was that, apparently, after Walker fled to England from Canada in 1990 to escape allegations of financial fraud, he and Ronald Platt had become friends and business partners. In 1992, Walker persuaded Platt to sell him his identity and move to Canada. But when Platt returned to England in 1995, Walker felt that the cover he had created for himself was threatened. At his trial in 1998, Albert Walker was found guilty of murder and sentenced to life in prison.

Water is a fundamental requirement of life, for both animals and plants. Without it, we would survive for no more than a few days. Access to safe drinking water is one of the major factors that divides the more-developed and less-developed nations of the world. But as well as being essential to life, water is responsible for what is estimated to be more than a quarter of a million *recorded* deaths by drowning worldwide every year.

The first question that usually needs to be answered when a body is found in water is: 'Did the person die in the water or were they already dead when they entered it?' Then, 'If they died in the water, was it because the water entered their lungs, or did they die from some other cause, such as cardiac arrest, vagal inhibition or laryngeal spasm – so-called dry drowning?'

Establishing the cause of death is the preserve of the forensic pathologist, who will look for classical signs of drowning, including changes in the size and texture of the lungs and the presence of foamy fluid in the air passages. Such signs are often transient and can become confused by the effects of decomposition or attempts at resuscitation. And it is in these sorts of complex circumstances that forensic scientists are often asked to help.

Perhaps the most useful type of scientific analysis in terms of cause of death in these circumstances is examination of body samples for the presence of microscopic algae called diatoms. Diatoms are characterised particularly by their siliceous (opaline) cell walls. It is their overall size and the shape and sculpturing of their cell walls that tell you what species you are dealing with. There is no accurate account of how many different sorts of diatoms exist, but rough estimates suggest that there are anything up to a million different species.

Diatoms exist in water or waterlogged ground in a wide variety of different forms, which vary from one location to another. If a person is alive when they enter water and inhale it, diatoms will enter their lungs and then travel in the circulation to other parts of the body, such as the liver and brain. If, on the other hand, the person is dead when they enter the water, and is therefore unable to inhale and has no circulation, any diatoms that do enter the lungs through the main airways will remain there.

So, by analysing body samples, it is possible to distinguish between death due to drowning and a body having been placed in water after death occurred. Also, if someone drowned in one location and was found in another, this is likely to be apparent through a mismatch in the types and proportions of the different diatoms found.

Take, for example, the case of an unidentified woman whose body was found at the mouth of an estuary. Diatoms recovered from the body indicated that she had drowned in fresh water, rather than in brackish water or the sea. When her identity was established, her home was found to be some 60 km (37 miles) upstream from where she was found and, following enquiries, it was suggested that she had drowned near her home.

It isn't just in cases of drowning that useful evidence can be derived from diatoms. In one case in which forensic biologist and diatom expert Dr Anthony Peabody gave evidence, a young man had been arrested for house burglary, which he denied. While examining the crime scene, a keen-eyed scenes of crime officer noticed a footwear mark leading to an ornamental garden pond and a wall, over which it was apparent that the intruder had made his escape. When Anthony examined the suspect's trousers, he found diatoms on the lower parts of them that were an exact match with the diatoms in the pond.

Aside from diatoms, what is also often helpful in determining precisely what happened in a case of suspected drowning is an analysis of samples of the person's blood and urine for drugs and alcohol. The presence of either or both of these substances at high levels might suggest an alternative cause of death, or could be a contributing factor to the predicament in which they found themselves. Any injuries the person may have suffered may also be relevant, particularly if these are indicative of restraint by someone else.

It is usually important to discover precisely where the person entered the water, which can be aided by local and professional knowledge of waterways and currents. Once the point of entry has been identified, marks such as tyre tracks or footwear marks in mud at the water's edge could hold critical clues as to how the person got there and who might have been with them. Signs of a struggle and drag marks might indicate what happened. Clothes and other discarded items, such as a weapon or cigarette end, may provide important links. And digital evidence from CCTV footage and/or mobile-phone data may prove useful.

Water can also be important in other types of investigation in terms of the damage it can cause. One example is in relation to the death in 1982 of the Italian banker Roberto Calvi, who was found suspended from some scaffolding under Blackfriars Bridge in London. Part of our re-investigation into his death some years later focused on the extent to which items he was wearing or were in the pockets of his clothing had been affected by the river water. This was important because, in conjunction with information about tide heights, currents and boat traffic, it helped in determining at what time of day he might have been suspended.

In another case at the other end of the scale, someone was suspected of trying to flush various items down the lavatory after the arrival of the police at a public house. The items in question were some herbal cannabis and fifteen small polythene bags, cannabis resin and four small polythene bags, another piece of cannabis resin with some clingfilm, forty-five small polythene bags inside a larger one, a lock knife, and a leather wallet containing banknotes.

The defendant denied the allegation, so the issue this time was about whether or not the items had ever been wet. With regard to the wallet, features such as the dull appearance of the leather, loss of texturing marks on the imitation silk lining, and dyestuff that appeared to have leached out of it on to the edges of some of the banknotes were a bit of a giveaway. Whitish salt deposits (from dried water) on some of the polythene bags, and mouldiness and staining from some of the cannabis on the bags, indicated that they, too, had been in water at some point.

Presumably the reason why our opinion was sought by the defence lawyer in this case was because there was some dispute about the condition of the items in question when they were found, and about the evidence supporting this from the scientist who first examined them.

Some criminals appear to think that disposing of incriminating items in water is a good idea as part of their strategy to evade detection. But, like other methods of disposal or concealment, this often simply creates more evidential traces for scientists to find, and provides more information about the criminals' activities.

12

Glass and paint

It was the early hours of the morning, and a party was being held on the thirteenth floor of a building in Leyton, east London, when a man wearing a face mask kicked a fire-bomb into the flat. In the panic that ensued, 26-year-old Donna O'Dwyer fell to her death from a balcony.

The electricity supply had failed immediately after the fire started, and investigation revealed that a wired-glass panel in a cupboard outside the flat had been broken in order to gain access to and cut the mains cable. Later that same day, police arrested a 34-year-old British Telecom engineer called Peter Thurston, who lived in a flat four floors below the one where the fire had occurred.

Among the evidential items that were subsequently seized from the suspect's flat was a pair of bolt croppers. When these were examined by one of the prosecution's forensic scientists at the MPFSL, fragments of glass were found embedded in one of the handles. It was stated in the forensic report that these could have come from the broken glass panel in the door of the electricity cupboard.

We were asked by the defendant's lawyer to look at the forensic report compiled for the prosecution. So my colleague Dr Clive Candy went to the police laboratory, where he examined the bolt croppers, together with a sample of glass and a cut piece of cable, which had been found in the cupboard outside the flat.

It was Clive's opinion that the minute fragments of glass that had been removed from some scratches in the blue paint close to the top of the handle of the bolt croppers *could*, indeed, have come from the broken glass panel. But as they were too small for the specific type of object they had come from to be identified, there was nothing to help confirm this. Establishing their refractive index and chemical composition didn't help either, because the same properties that are found in window glass can also be found in items such as glass ashtrays and light bulbs.

Also, of course, it wasn't possible to know *when* the glass had become embedded in the bolt croppers. According to the scientist who did the original forensic investigation, the fragments looked clean, bright and sharp, and there was nothing to indicate that they had been worn down or become dirty with age. Although Clive agreed in principle with him on this point, he stated in his report that it wasn't clear how the embedded glass *would* have become worn down. What he also said was that an alternative explanation for the fragments not having collected dirt might be that the bolt croppers hadn't been used frequently, or that they had been stored unused for a long period of time.

The distance from the scratches in the handle of the bolt croppers to the tip of their cutting blades was six inches (15 cm). The police had taken photographs of the electricity cupboard door when the broken glass panel and cut cable were still *in situ*. And what also caught Clive's attention when he examined these was that the distance between the cable and the glass panel when the door was closed also appeared to be approximately six inches. So if the blades of the bolt croppers had been positioned over the cable when the cut was made, the broken wired glass in the door would have been approximately six inches from their tip, and in the same position as the scratches in which the embedded glass had been found.

The defendant's lawyer obviously hoped that Clive would be able to cast doubt on some aspect of the prosecution's evidence. But, in fact, Clive concluded that the bolt croppers found in Peter Thurston's flat were 'more likely than not to have been the tool that severed the electricity cable outside Flat 135'.

At his trial at the Old Bailey in September 1995, Peter Thurston was convicted of murder, arson and causing grievous bodily harm – apparently because he was annoyed by his noisy neighbours – and he was jailed for life.

This forensically relatively simple case illustrates how the power of trace evidence, such as tiny fragments of glass, can be transformed by an understanding of precisely where they were found – in this instance, embedded in scratches on the surface of a pair of bolt croppers exactly six inches from their blade tips. Just as 'every contact leaves a trace', 'context is everything' when it comes to understanding what that trace might mean.

Most types of glass are made from similar raw materials, essentially silica sand, soda ash (sodium bicarbonate) and limestone (calcium carbonate). So you might think that one fragment of broken glass would be much like any other. But because the proportions of the raw materials vary according to what the glass is going to be used for, and different glasses can contain different natural impurities, an experienced forensic scientist can deduce quite a lot about a shard of broken glass from the chemical analysis of its constituents. The glass used to make windows, for example, contains iron oxide, which gives it a green tinge when viewed side on. But because no one would want to drink milk that appears to be a rather unappetising shade of green, all the iron is removed from glass destined to be made into milk bottles by using iron-free sand.

These different chemical compositions, together with the way glass is heated and cooled during the production process, give them different refractive indices. (The refractive index is basically a measure of how much a substance can 'bend' light – think of sticks in water.)

One method of producing sheets of clear, colourless glass that don't distort your view when you look through them – window glass, for example – is the float process. This involves 'floating' the molten glass across the surface of a bath of molten tin. As the glass crosses the molten metal, then cools and is drawn off at the other end, tiny particles of tin become adsorbed on to the surface that has been in contact with it. It is the fact that these particles of tin fluoresce a light-green colour when seen under short-wave ultraviolet light that makes float glass identifiable.

In order to produce heat-toughened glass such as that used in low-level glazing in buildings – patio doors and the side and rear windows of cars, for instance – cold air is directed on to both sides of the sheet so that the outer 'skin' of glass cools first, leaving the interior still hot. Then, when the interior also cools and contracts, the outer layer on each side is compressed, making it more difficult to break.

The physical appearance of even a tiny fragment of glass might tell you what sort of object it probably came from. For instance, flat pieces of glass are quite likely to have come from a pane. Any slight curvature in the glass – providing it is an original surface – would indicate that it could be from a container of some sort, such as a drinking glass or bottle. Measuring the thickness of a fragment of glass with both its original surfaces present can also reflect what it was used for. And general grime on one surface and not on the other will indicate which side has been exposed to the elements and which side hasn't.

These technical details are important to forensic scientists for various reasons. For example, by comparing the appearance, refractive index and chemical composition of slivers of glass found on a suspect's clothing, they can show that these *could* have come from a broken pane of glass in the door of premises that have been broken into. However, unless the glass in the door has some unusual distinguishing properties, it is rarely possible to say that it *must* have done so.

Where several panes of a multi-paned window or door have been broken, glass analysis can provide a very strong association with the person responsible. This is because the different panes very often have different chemical and physical properties, and the combination of results from a number of different panes can increase the value of the evidential link exponentially.

Glass fragments commonly comprise part of the forensic evidence in crimes that start with breaking and entering. And as these types of crime often involve breaking through windows and doors, forensic scientists will also look for flakes of paint.

To the naked eye, one fragment of white paint might look pretty much like any other. But it is surprising what an experienced forensic scientist can discover by examining and comparing flakes of paint using specialist high-power microscopes, sometimes supported by detailed chemical analysis.

Of course, paint comes in all sorts of different types and colours. Where a surface has been painted repeatedly over a period of time, however, and especially when different colours have been used, a sequence of layers will have built up, which will be reflected in any flakes that are chipped off it. So colour tends to feature prominently in paint comparisons.

Paint is a mixture of several different components with different functions. These include binders (as a basis), pigments (for colour), extenders (for coverage and strength) and modifiers (to impart specific characteristics such as gloss and weather resistance). The nature and proportion of these organic and inorganic chemical substances will reflect how the paint was made and what it was to be used for. Was it an undercoat or topcoat? To be used on a building or a vehicle? Outdoors or inside?

Paint examinations therefore begin with a detailed inspection under the microscope of reference samples of paint from the crime scene, for example. The overall layer structure and then the appearance of the individual layers are examined, before being compared with paint samples from the suspect, vehicle, tool or whatever else is thought to be related to the crime. Features of interest will include the colours, thicknesses, textures and spread of any particles within the respective layers. More detailed assessments of colour can then be made, using a microspectrophotometer (MSP), and of chemical composition, usually with a scanning electron microscope fitted with an electron microprobe.

When two brothers were arrested on suspicion of stealing property from a ground-floor flat in London, they were taken to a local police station, where their clothing was seized. Entry to the flat had been gained by breaking a wooden panel in the door. And when a sharp-eyed police officer noticed a flake of white paint in the hood of the anorak taken from one of the suspects, it was gathered up with the flake carefully preserved inside it.

The clothing of both suspects was subsequently examined at the MPFSL, where the flake of paint found in the hood was compared with a sample taken from the broken door panel. What the forensic scientist discovered when she examined the wooden panel was that one side of it had been painted with three layers of white paint, while the other side had five layers of white paint, covered by four layers of varnish.

After removing samples of the paint and varnish from the wood, the MPFSL scientist used a range of specialist microscopes to compare them with the paint flake from the hood of the suspect's anorak. What she found was that the single paint flake from the hood and two fragments of paint found in the suspect's shirt pocket all matched the white-paint-and-varnished side of the broken wooden panel. This was confirmed by a second comparison that involved staining the paint with the chemical rhodamine which causes individual layers of white paint to become coloured different shades of pink, according to how well they take up the stain.

When we were asked by the suspect's solicitor to check the prosecution's forensic evidence, my colleague Clive Candy examined the paint flakes that had been recovered from the anorak and shirt. Then he compared them microscopically, as the original forensic scientist had done, with the paint from the broken panel. What Clive concluded was that although the combination of layers of paint on the panel could not be considered to be unique to the flat, it would be extremely unlikely to find another source that would match in all the tests that had been applied.

Having excluded any obvious route of accidental contamination, it was therefore Clive's opinion that the link between the suspect and the scene of the burglary was highly significant. The evidence was also strengthened by the fact that the paint flakes had been found in the hood of the suspect's anorak and the pocket of his shirt – which is exactly where you might expect them to become trapped if the method of entry to the flat had involved crawling through the broken panel in the door, as suggested by the prosecution.

One of the things I particularly like about this case is that it involved 'plain old' white paint. Just imagine what forensic scientists can do with multi-layered coloured paint!

Sometimes, paint can be found not as flakes, but in the form of smears when there has been forceful contact with a painted surface. For example, collisions between vehicles often result in smears of paint being transferred between them. Smears of paint from a car can also be found on the clothing of a victim of a hit-and-run incident in which it has been involved. This is often supported by other evidence, such as tyre marks and engine oil on the victim's clothing, and their blood, textile fibres and fabric impressions of their clothing on the vehicle. Crushed paint can be found on the ends of jemmies and other tools used for break-ins, where it may be associated with tool marks left on the painted surface. And spray paint used for graffiti produces tiny spots of paint, some of which can drift back on to the hands and clothing of the writer/painter and provide evidence of their involvement.

We have considered just two types of trace here, but there is an almost infinite variety of others that can potentially provide evidence to connect people, places, the vehicles they use and the objects they handle. The trick with traces is to work out what you might expect in a given set of circumstances and focus on those aspects, while at the same time taking notice of anything else that might conceivably offer completely unexpected links or insights into the crime. Sometimes, these are far more powerful than the more traditional types of trace that you originally had in your sights.

13

Knives and firearms

There are many ways in which people can injure each other, with and without a weapon: by punching, kicking, stamping and headbutting, as well as with poisons, blunt instruments, knives and firearms. The most common weapons used in violent attacks are probably knives, and the most common knife crimes involve assault, with robbery a close second. According to Home Office statistics, after having declined for several years, knife crime in England and Wales* rose by 80 per cent between 2014 and 2019, to a total of 43,516 during the year ending March 2019.† Between 2017 and 2018 (which is the last year for which the numbers are available), there were 285 knife-related killings in England and Wales, the majority of them in London.

During the last ten to twenty years, stabbing has also increasingly played a role in terrorist attacks. These often involve offenders strapping knives to their wrists and running amok, attempting to kill or injure as many people as possible before they are stopped. Such crimes have occurred in numerous countries and territories, including Britain, Germany, Australia, the West Bank, the USA and France.

* The statistics for Scotland and Northern Ireland are compiled separately, as the collection of crime data is slightly different in these countries.
† Due to recording issues, this figure excludes data from Greater Manchester Police.

In one such case, which took place in London on 29 November 2019, five people were stabbed by Usman Khan, a convicted terrorist who had been released on licence halfway through a sixteen-year prison sentence. Khan had been attending an offender rehabilitation conference at Fishmongers' Hall when he threatened to detonate a suicide vest that he indicated he was wearing. With two kitchen knives strapped to his wrists, he then immediately started attacking people, including two young conference organisers, who subsequently died.

Several other people, among them ex-prisoners, prison officers and Fishmongers' Hall staff, armed themselves with whatever was to hand. With 'weapons' that included a fire extinguisher, a pole, chairs and a narwhal tusk, they managed to drive Khan out of the building on to London Bridge. He was then apprehended, restrained and partially disarmed by police and members of the public before additional officers arrived and he was shot dead.

Following the attack, London Bridge was closed for several hours to allow the crime scene to be investigated and recorded. An appeal was also issued for members of the public to submit any footage they might have taken of the incident. The response that was received allowed the sequence of events to be pieced together properly, both for the inquests into the deaths of those who had been killed, and to ensure that any lessons for the future could be learned.

While there had been plenty of eyewitnesses and some of the action had been captured on mobile phones, it was still necessary for the weapons and some other items to be submitted to a forensic laboratory for confirmatory testing. Without the impartial factual information this provides, it is possible for misinterpretations and misunderstandings to seep into evidence and infect court proceedings.

There are various reasons for the relatively common use of knives in violent attacks. They are easily available, both for purchase in shops and being present in every home and many office and industrial environments. Anyone can use a knife as an offensive weapon without requiring any training. A knife can be easily transported and concealed in a bag, pocket or the waistband of a pair of trousers. And, compared to the use of other types of weapon, the punishment for knife crime in the UK is currently quite limited, although sentences are increasing – presumably in response to its increasing prevalence.

Knives come in a wide variety of types: the full range of kitchen knives, personal knives such as penknives, lock and larger pocket knives, flick knives, butterfly knives (which have a handle in two parts that close over the blade when not in use), hunting knives (which usually have very sharp, rigid blades and are therefore kept in sheaths), machetes (which have a broad blade), military knives such as bayonets, and ceremonial knives such as daggers and swords.

The number of cuts inflicted in a knife attack varies from just one or two to a multitude in the sort of frenzied attack that results when the offender loses control. Another variable is the amount of blood found on the knife afterwards, which can range from none, or only tiny traces that aren't visible to the naked eye, to heavy staining that covers both the blade and the handle. This depends on various factors, including the number of cuts inflicted, the part of the body affected and the depth of penetration of the knife.

Also important are the nature and thickness of any clothing through which the knife has had to pass, and the extent to which this wiped off the blood as the knife blade was withdrawn. It will also be affected by whether the victim tried to defend themselves with unclothed hands or arms, and, of course, whether any attempt was made after the attack to clean the knife.

An additional aspect in any knife attack is the possibility that the person wielding the knife will injure themselves. This can happen when the weapon is turned back on the attacker by the intended victim during a struggle. It can also occur when the blade becomes slippery with blood, causing the attacker's hand to slide down from the handle on to the cutting edge of the blade. In the case of a folding knife such as a penknife, an attacker may also be injured if the blade folds over their fingers. For the forensic scientist, this last aspect is actually very important, because it means that the attacker's blood and DNA may be detectable on the victim or elsewhere at the crime scene or beyond (in a getaway car, for example), thereby potentially providing good evidence of their involvement.

When seized for examination, great care is always taken not to disturb any tiny traces of what may prove to be evidence on the surface of the knife. One way of achieving this is to put it in a type of plastic tube that was specially designed to hold a knife securely in place and ensure that it does not come into contact with the walls of the tube, which could cause minute evidential traces to be dislodged. Such traces might commonly include dried blood from the victim, and possibly from the attacker, as well as hairs, textile fibres and fingerprints from either or both.

Back at the forensic laboratory, the knife is carefully examined under a microscope for any particulate matter such as hairs and textile fibres. If present, these are picked off with a pair of fine forceps, with great care being taken not to disturb any fingerprints, glove prints or other marks in the process. They will then be securely mounted for future detailed examination under a microscope.

What the microscope examination will also establish is whether there is any blood on the knife. As with just about anything with blood on it, the nature and distribution of blood on a knife can often provide an experienced scientist with additional information about how it got there. For example, a sharp, horizontal demarcation of blood part of the way down the blade can indicate how far into the victim's body it penetrated. Bloodstaining confined to the cutting edge of the blade can indicate that the knife was used in a slashing, as opposed to stabbing, motion. And heavy blood-staining on the handle of a knife can suggest that the perpetrator of the attack was also injured. Attempts to clean blood off the knife may also be apparent, yielding further potentially useful information.

Once all evidential traces have been meticulously recorded and removed, and/or appropriate samples have been taken of them, the forensic scientist's attention will turn to aspects of the knife itself. These include its overall size, the length and width of its blade and whether it has been bent, whether the blade is single- or double-edged, and the sharpness of the cutting edge or edges. These are all critical details when comparing a specific knife with the nature and dimensions of wounds in the victim's body and cuts in their clothing, and when considering what might have happened during the dynamic events of the attack.

It is only at this stage of the forensic examination – once all potential evidential samples have been removed from the blade – that test cuts can be made with the knife, usually in a specially prepared 'stabbing box'. As with every other aspect of forensic investigations, getting as near the real thing as possible is key to this sort of testing. So if the examination of the victim's clothing has been completed, an unaffected part of it may be spread over the stabbing box and stabbed into. The test cuts are then clearly marked to avoid any possible confusion with the cuts made during the crime.

Investigating the track of the knife through successive layers of the victim's clothing can indicate the position the victim was in when he or she was struck, with respect to the knife and therefore the person wielding it. (This is also true of the knife tracks in the victim's body, of course, but it is the patholo-gist who will deal with those.) To assist in this process by lining up the cuts in successive items, forensic scientists some-times place the victim's clothing on a dummy. Digital recon-structions can also help with this type of analysis, and can make the information more accessible to investigators and, later on, the court.

But it isn't only the victim's clothing that can tell a story. Cuts (and blood) in clothing belonging to the suspect can also be important. For example, cuts in the pocket of a jacket or pair of trousers might suggest that this is where a knife was carried, while a cut in the lower front of upper clothing might indicate that a knife had been tucked into the waistband.

Like knives, firearms also come in all shapes, sizes and functionalities. Although some types of firearm are more popular than others, they can all be used in the commission of crime.

In one case we were involved with, a man had walked into a newsagent and robbed the shopkeeper at gunpoint. During the robbery, the shotgun went off, killing the shopkeeper. The suspect said that he had been holding the gun at arm's length and pointing it at the shopkeeper, who was 16–20 feet (5–6 m) away, when his accomplice, who was outside the shop, pushed open the door on to him, causing the gun to fire accidentally. So the case hinged on the range from which the shopkeeper had been shot.

Close inspection of the body revealed a mark in the shape of a Maltese cross close to the wound site. By doing a series of test fires in the laboratory, it was established that this had been made by contact with the petals of the cartridge wad, which had opened up on firing to form the cross pattern. The tests also showed that the muzzle of the gun could have been no more than 18–24 inches (46–61 cm) away from the shop-keeper at the time. In other words, the suspect could not have been standing by the door, as he claimed, but must rather have been up against the shop counter.

Apparently, the shooter told his father what he had done and where he had abandoned the gun. And when the weapon was recovered from the River Thames, it was possible to match the wad to the barrel from the striations that had been created when it was sawn off. Having put himself at the scene of the crime with the gun, and having admitted to the shooting, the suspect was convicted of killing the shopkeeper.

There are numerous indicators resulting from the discharge of a firearm that can help forensic scientists to establish factors such as the range – as in the case above – and angle of muzzle to the impact point. For example, when a gun is fired, the FDRs that are forced down and out of the barrel can provide range indicators that include skin and hair searing, soot deposits and stippling (tattooing): the greater the area of stippling, the greater the range. Escape of some of the FDRs can also cause contamination of surfaces close to the point of escape that can help to establish whether a person has recently discharged, handled or been in close proximity to a discharged firearm.

In the year ending 31 March 2019, 6,759 firearm offences were recorded in England and Wales, which was a slight increase on the previous year. In the year 2019–20, 552 illegal firearms were seized as a result of work done by the National Crime Agency. So gun crime is an important aspect of the investigations that are carried out by forensic scientists.

Although the prevalence of gun crime in the UK is one of the lowest in the world, reducing the criminal use of firearms by organised crime groups, terrorists and urban gangs is a priority for law enforcement. Most of the gun crime committed in the UK is by street gangs involved in drug distribution and armed robberies, and many of the victims are already known to the police. The majority of illegal firearms are smuggled in from Central and Eastern Europe, often entering from France hidden in vehicles on Channel ferries and travelling through the tunnel. A few are sold on the dark web and enter by post in parcels; and some are stolen from lawful owners.

The Firearms Act 1968 defines a firearm as 'A lethal barrelled weapon of any description from which any shot, bullet or other missile can be discharged.' These weapons include air firearms, which use compressed air or other gases to shoot a projectile, and non-air firearms, which rely on the chemical compression of gases to fire combustible propellants.

Probably the most common non-air firearms involved in crimes are handguns such as pistols and revolvers, which normally discharge single projectiles – bullets. Historically, shotguns have been a popular choice for criminals and are still used in a number of crimes. Shotguns usually discharge multiple projectiles in the form of lead pellets (known as shot).

There are various elements related to guns, their pellets, bullets and cartridge cases that provide important evidence for the forensic scientist. For example, the markings in the metal on the bottom of a cartridge case can indicate its type and/or manufacturer. Impressions left by the gun's firing pin on the primer of a spent cartridge case, together with any extractor and ejector marks, can indicate what type of gun fired it. Measuring bullets will indicate the calibre – i.e. the internal diameter of the barrel – of the gun from which they have been fired. Bullets fired from handguns and rifles pick up the patterns of spiral grooves that are cut on the inside of the barrel to impart spin to the bullets as they are projected through it. These rifling characteristics can be compared with information on databases to indicate possible models of firearm used. Also, the tools used to manufacture the rifling within the barrels leave microscopic marks, known as toolmarks, which are unique and may be identifiable from databases in order to establish bullet-to-gun and crime-to-crime links.

The number of bullets found at a crime scene and inside a victim's body, together with any signs of damage to them caused by impact and ricochet, can help indicate how many shots were fired, the actual trajectory of the bullets, and therefore where the shooter was likely to have been positioned. The nature and location of the wounds on a victim, as well as the blood patterns associated with them, can help to establish the range at which the shots were fired, the relative position of victim and shooter at the time, and often something about the overall sequence of events.

In one of the many cases forensic firearms expert Geoff Arnold has worked on, he was asked to examine the ballistic evidence relating to a suspected murder in Kenya. On 4 June 2016, Grace Wangechi Kinyanjui was fatally shot in the house of a man called Richard Alden. One of the elements that led to Alden being arrested and charged with her murder was the misinterpretation of the ballistic wounds.

It had been thought that evidential wounds to the hand of the deceased were defence wounds related to a bladed weapon. But incident reconstruction, test firing into ballistic simulant (designed to simulate the soft tissues of the body), and associated calculations proved that they were actually ballistic wounds. These had been inflicted by the bullet after it had exited her body and when her hand had been over the exit wound in the neck area when the firearm was discharged. In fact, the fatal wound had been accidentally self-inflicted as the result of an unintended discharge and ricochet.

Using the wide range of characteristics of different knives, firearms and ammunition, it is possible for forensic scientists to amass a lot of very valuable information about the specific nature of the weapon involved in a case and precisely how it was used. Traces such as fingerprints, and DNA from blood or contact, can then often confirm links with particular victims and identify likely perpetrators of the crime.

14

CCTV and other digital evidence

The result of some forensic analysis, especially DNA with its powerful statistics, often needs to be backed up by at least one other type of evidence before the court can be sufficiently satisfied to convict – or acquit – a suspect of a crime. That back-up evidence has increasingly included digital information derived from CCTV cameras, mobile phones and computers. But digital devices often provide critical evidence in their own right, as in one case we worked on when it was a combination of CCTV footage and a trail of bloody footwear marks that helped to solve a crime involving a violent attack on the owner of a sex shop in Bournemouth.

When Adam Shaw's body was discovered in his shop, there were many bloodstained footwear marks on the floor. Although it was possible to establish the approximate size of the shoes that had produced the marks, interrogation of manufacturers' databases failed to provide any information about which firm had made them. What could be established, however, was that after entering the shop, locking the door and stabbing his victim multiple times, the attacker had left the premises by climbing out into the garden through a small window at the back, around the edges of which were discovered some purple polyester fibres.

When footage from a nearby CCTV camera was examined, it showed a man walking along the street at around the time the attack was thought to have taken place wearing a striking purple top under his jacket. The brand name on the uppers of the man's shoes was clearly visible. And once the manufacturer had been identified, it was confirmed that the soles of the shoes had the same pattern as the bloodstained marks at the crime scene.

Even that information might not have been enough to move the investigation forward, however, if it hadn't been for the fact that that particular make and type of shoe was only available by mail order. Even more fortuitously, just a small number of people in the area had bought the shoes in the size range that had been established from the footwear marks at the crime scene. So it was a relatively simple matter for the police to visit all of them – until they came across a man who bore a very close resemblance to the man wearing a purple top in the CCTV footage.

Having identified the man and visited him at his home, police officers searched the property and removed various items of clothing, including a leather jacket. And although they didn't find a purple fleece, forensic biologist Roy Green did find purple fibres inside the leather jacket that matched those discovered around the window at the crime scene.

Faced with the various strands of scientific evidence when the case went to court, nineteen-year-old Terry Gibbs pleaded guilty to the murder of Adam Shaw and was sentenced to life in prison.

While some forces do all their own CCTV analysis work, others contract some or all of it out to private companies. This includes cleaning up and, where necessary, enhancing footage to clarify it and identify those involved; scanning it for anything of potential relevance to a specific crime; and logging particular features of interest.

According to the Office for National Statistics, there are approximately 13,900 CCTV cameras in public spaces in

London alone. The number drops significantly outside the capital, with Bristol being in second place with 658. But there are also many other cameras on company premises, including restaurants, bars and other places of entertainment, and increasingly at private addresses. So one of the first things the police now do at crime scenes is find out where the nearest CCTV cameras are and check the footage on them, as happened in a case involving one of the sons of the former Ugandan dictator Idi Amin.

Faisal Wangita was part of a gang who savagely attacked and killed an eighteen-year-old Somali engineering student called Mahir Osman in Camden Town, London, in January 2006. Osman – who was a member of a rival gang – was attacked with a variety of weapons, including baseball bats, bottles and hammers, and was also punched, kicked and stabbed with a knife more than twenty times.

A security guard had been monitoring the CCTV on his firm's premises when he noticed that people were starting to gather together in the street outside. When the footage was later viewed by police, those people turned out to be members of the gang who set upon Osman after having forced him off a bus. Pushing him to the ground at the back of the bus, they subjected him to a severe and sustained attack: at one point, the video footage showed feathers billowing out of his Puffa jacket as he was stabbed. The gang then got back on the bus and it drove off, just as the blue lights of pursuing police cars became apparent.

When the police stopped the bus, gang members could be seen climbing out through its windows as they tried to get away. A group of them assaulted a passer-by, pinning him up against some railings while one of them went through his pockets – which was again captured on camera.

A substantial number of the gang members were apprehended by the police, and CCTV footage from various cameras proved invaluable in helping to identify what had happened, who had been directly involved in the attack – by matching images of their clothing – and what part they had played in it. It also provided clues to where might be the best places to take samples for DNA profiling as supporting evidence. In forensic terms, it was a massive case, involving hundreds of items for examination and analysis.

In 2007, three of the gang members were jailed for life for murder. Eleven more were given prison sentences for offences connected to the incident, including Faisal Wangita, who was sentenced to five years for conspiracy to wound, conspiracy to possess offensive weapons and violent disorder. Four years later, the fifteenth person to be convicted in relation to the killing was sentenced to at least sixteen years in prison.

According to one senior police officer, the premeditated attack on Mahir Osman involved a level of violence he had rarely seen. Another officer said that more needed to be done to stop street gangs being formed by young men such as those who had taken part in the attack.

Sometimes, even when the identity of the perpetrator of a crime is in little doubt, CCTV footage can still prove useful in understanding the course of events and exactly what happened. One horrific example was a case involving a man who went on a killing spree, which, within the space of just a few hours, left twelve people dead and eleven injured.

In the early hours of the morning of 2 June 2010, 52-year-old taxi driver Derrick Bird left his home in the village of Rowrah in Cumbria, in north-west England, and drove a few miles to the home of his twin brother, David. After shooting his brother several times, CCTV footage showed Derrick Bird driving to a farmhouse that belonged to a solicitor called Kevin Commons where, according to numerous witnesses, he remained outside for about the next four hours. By the time police arrived at the farmhouse shortly after 10 a.m., having been alerted by reports of shots being fired, Kevin Commons had been shot in the head and shoulder and was lying dead outside his home.

It was a difficult day for Cumbria Police, as their firearms team was apparently busy fifty miles (80 km) away policing the Appleby Horse Fair. But RAF helicopters joined what soon became a massive police hunt.

By 11.30 that morning, Bird had shot twenty-three people, twelve of whom had been killed, while eleven, including three of his fellow taxi drivers, survived with various degrees of injury. After abandoning his car and one of his guns, Bird then continued on foot armed with a rifle. And at 1.30 p.m., his body was found in an area of woodland some twenty miles (32 km) from his home.

Apparently, in the period preceding that terrible day, Bird had been feeling increasingly socially isolated. And after becoming convinced that his brother and solicitor had been plotting against him, it was shooting them that sparked the other shootings.

In terms of digital forensics, specialists in the firm Acume, led by director and former West Yorkshire Police officer Stephen Cole, had been commissioned to build a narrative with an interactive map for each of the victims. This involved setting out their individual interactions with Bird and where the police and other emergency services were at the time. As well as footage from a wide variety of sources, including thirty cameras in one street alone, the investigators also used a considerable amount of domestic footage. The narratives they created, which were subsequently presented at the inquest, painted a picture of what had happened for the victims' families, as though Bird was on trial in the dock.

It is surprisingly common for such narratives to be commissioned to help the court understand the sequence of events if this has been protracted and at least some of it captured on camera. But, of course, care has to be taken to stick to the facts and not make assumptions to cover any gaps in the record.

Digital forensics isn't all about CCTV footage though. The examination of mobile-phone data by digital forensic examiners can also help to solve a wide variety of types of cases. One such case involved a well-known sports personality suspected of breaching industry betting rules and regulations. When the data files from his mobile phone were analysed, they revealed lengthy conversations that he'd had with several individuals, which resulted in him being charged by the sporting body, and subsequently admitting to a number of betting-related offences.

In another case, digital forensic specialists were involved in supporting a UK-based law enforcement agency with an investigation into offences related to child abuse and the production of indecent images of children. After extracting data from multiple devices – including mobile phones – at a number of premises, they identified one particular smartphone at one location that contained a huge quantity of indecent images of children, together with various other important evidential items. After evidence was discovered of ongoing child sexual abuse in the US, a suspect was arrested and is now serving a custodial sentence. Another twenty-three suspects have also been identified worldwide as part of what is, at the time of writing, an ongoing operation. Over the past two decades, this particular case of online child abuse has turned out to be a much larger problem than was initially suspected, and it currently occupies many digital forensics specialists in this country and across the world.

It isn't just what's recorded *on* individual mobile phones that can be of interest in criminal investigations, but also where the user of the phone was at critical times, and with whom they might have been communicating. This sort of information is obtained by combining analysis of call-data records from phone service providers with cell-site data. While different networks vary, call-data records provide logs of the date, time and duration of each call made or text message sent, and the individual number(s) called. Cell-site data tells you which cell on which transmitting mast (cell site) facilitated the call/message. And because the networks work on the 'best serving cell principle', this also tells you whereabouts the phone must have been at the time, although this always has to be checked by individual survey measurement.

As with everything forensic, you have to be careful that digital evidence means what you think it means. One case that highlighted this involved someone accused of burglary whom a police analyst said was 'in the vicinity' of the crime at the time. This seemed to be potentially powerful circumstantial evidence, until a closer analysis on behalf of the defence of the sorts of records described above demonstrated that the suspect had a similar pattern of cell-site use during the previous four nights in a row, and also for the night after the burglary. Moreover, a survey indicated that the cell involved didn't even point towards the crime scene. And when the suspect said he had been at a valid location five miles (8 km) away, the Crown offered no evidence and the case was dropped. This also highlights the fact that – again, as with other types of forensic evidence – it is always important not to take everything at face value: however large or small the case, the results will be very important to those involved.

With so much information now being stored on digital devices, the field of computer forensics has grown exponentially during the last few years. Digital devices such as computers, external hard drives, storage servers and memory cards can hold enormous amounts of data that can be critically important to investigators. As well as showing who has been in touch with whom, when and about what, this data can show what subjects have been researched, what items have been ordered online, and myriad other things that reflect the lives of those who have owned or used the devices. Even information that has been encrypted or subject to unusual operating systems can be extracted and analysed.

Also, of course, mobile phones and computer keyboards can prove to be very useful sources of the DNA of the people who have been using them. In fact, I can remember many years ago being a bit puzzled when we were asked to look at yet another keyboard for traces of semen, before realising that the potential crimes being investigated involved pornography. Nowadays, I think we're all much more aware than we were in those relatively early days of the internet.

Another aspect of digital forensics involves the computerised reconstructions that are sometimes used to show crime scenes and the possible course of events in complex cases. One fascinating example of this was the computerised enhancement in 2013 of camera footage from the 1913 Epsom Derby, which enabled an event that had occurred a century earlier to be seen in quite a different light.

Emily Wilding Davison was born in 1872, just as the fight for suffrage for women was becoming the focus of a national movement in England. After studying at Royal Holloway College in London and at Oxford University, Emily became a teacher. In 1906, as the demand for votes for women was gaining support and the suffragettes were becoming more militant, she joined the Women's Social and Political Union.

Three years later, Emily gave up her teaching job to work full time for the suffragette movement, and became involved in activities that resulted in her serving several short prison sentences. On 4 June 1913, she was knocked down and trampled on by King George V's horse after she had ducked under the railing and stepped on to the racecourse during the Epsom Derby.

It had always been assumed that Emily didn't have a clear view of the king's horse as it approached the area where she was standing among the crowd, and that her action had been intended to bring it down. But when the enhanced footage from three different camera angles was studied, it became apparent that she *was* able to see the horse before she stepped under the railing and on to the course.

During the four seconds that elapse before she is struck by the horse – apparently as it attempts to jump over her – Emily appears to watch it approach. She has something in her hand that looks like a scarf, and as she steps forward, she raises it as if to try to slip it on to the horse. Perhaps she misjudged the force of an animal of that size moving at that speed. But whatever her intention had been, the impact induced a coma and she died in hospital four days later.

In 1997, a silk scarf with the words 'Votes for Women' emblazoned on it was bought at an auction at Sotheby's in London. The seller of the scarf was the daughter of a man who had been clerk of the course at the Epsom Derby some seventy-four years earlier, when he had picked it up off the ground from beside the comatose body of Emily Wilding Davison.

Digital forensic specialists also investigate cybercrime, which includes any crime that involves computers, digital depositories of data from them, and networks that link them. Cybercrime can threaten the security and finances of individuals, companies, even entire nations. It involves breaches of the integrity of personal, industrial, commercial, academic and state information held in digital databanks, and use of this information, for example to blackmail people or steal their identities. Cybercrimes can also be transaction-based crimes such as fraud, counterfeiting, money laundering and trafficking in child pornography, as well as crimes committed by people within organisations, such as deleting or altering data for profit or political gain.

Challenges associated with cybercrime include the relative anonymity of perpetrators and the fact that they can operate globally from their personal computers. Cyberterrorism, which is at the extreme end of the spectrum, involves so-called 'hostile actors' attempting to disrupt use of the internet, or to use it to cause public disturbance and instability, even death.

Cybercrime experts specialise in investigating crime when it has occurred, and devising systems and processes to try to prevent it in the future. Obviously, the vast majority of this activity is digitally based. Some of the work is undertaken by private companies, but the more sensitive assignments are handled by government agencies.

It is second nature to most of us to protect our homes, property and businesses from criminal activity. We do this by fitting locks, alarm systems and, increasingly, CCTV; many businesses also have security patrols. But even though most of us now own computers and mobile phones, we often don't seem to take the same approach with our cyber-security, despite the fact that being the target of cybercrime may result in emotional trauma and financial ruin.

At the time of writing, changes to working practices resulting from the Covid-19 pandemic have provided unprecedented opportunities for cybercriminals to gain access to our data. As a result, there has recently been a spate of high-profile cases involving such well-known companies as Travelex and the Premier League.

Cyber-security statistics for 2020 reported by the company IT Governance list 1,120 breaches and cyber-attacks that resulted in the loss of 20.1 billion records of personal data. Quite apart from the effects on the organisations themselves – the full extent of which is not yet known – some of the individuals whose personal details were involved will have to deal with the effects of identity theft for the purpose of fraud and other criminal activity.

Ransomware attacks are one type of cybercrime that is proving increasingly popular with criminals. These involve perpetrators locking (encrypting) other people's data and only releasing it on payment of a ransom. The most important thing for victims of ransomware attacks to do is quickly isolate the device concerned by disconnecting it from the internet and any networks to reduce the risk of the ransomware spreading to other machines that share the same network.

Of course, prevention is better than cure, and using reputable, up-to-date anti-malware software and a firewall, and not opening any suspicious email links or attachments or responding to unsolicited emails, phone calls or text messages, should all help to provide protection.

The whole digital revolution has happened since the start of my career as a forensic scientist in the 1970s. Today, digital forensics is one of the three most requested forms of forensic testing, along with DNA and fingerprints.

15

Forgery and fraud

After 55-year-old David Napier Hamilton disappeared one day in November 1985, his lover, Kingsley Rotardier, explained his absence by telling people he was suffering from AIDS and had gone abroad. Over the next few months, David Napier Hamilton's credit card was used and various letters were received by his friends, supposedly from him, explaining that he had gone away for treatment. But in January 1986, Rotardier was tried and found guilty of fraudulent use of David Napier Hamilton's credit card and sentenced to nine months in prison. As soon as the trial was over, he was re-arrested and charged with murder.

The various letters, together with some examples of business writing of David Napier Hamilton's taken from his work, were submitted for analysis at the Metropolitan Police Forensic Science Laboratory. When the items were examined by 'questioned document' examiner Chris Davies, he found that although the handwriting of the letters was pictorially similar to David Napier Hamilton's, it was of much poorer quality – which would be expected if it was a copy.

The complicating factor was that if David Napier Hamilton did have AIDS, as claimed by Rotardier, there was no information about the effect this might have on his handwriting, and whether it could account for the poorer quality. However, there were some clear structural differences in character forms, and even if the quality of someone's writing might be affected by AIDS, there was no reason to believe that it would change the structure of only certain characters. The evidence therefore indicated that all the letters were copied handwriting. And although it wasn't possible to say by whom, there was other evidence that seemed to implicate Rotardier.

Among the items Rotardier had bought with David Napier Hamilton's credit card were a butcher's saw and cleaver, which the police began to suspect he might have used to cut up the body before burning it, bit by bit, in the garden. Indeed, neighbours had reported noxious smoke at around the relevant time. Also, some of David Napier Hamilton's friends who had received letters from him, in which he wrote of his shame about having AIDS, claimed that the phraseology seemed wrong and that he said things they were certain he would never have said, however ill he was.

At his trial for murder in January 1988, Kingsley Rotardier insisted that David Napier Hamilton was still alive and continuing to battle his illness in Malaysia. But although a body has never been found, the jury returned a verdict of guilty and he was sentenced to twenty years in prison.

Something that only came out after his trial was the fact that Rotardier had previously been suspected of murder while living in the US. When police had searched his house there, they had found clothing in the boot of his car that was soaked with blood, which turned out to match the blood of the victim. But because they only had a warrant to search the house and not the car, that evidence was ruled inadmissible and the case never went to trial. It was clearly unfortunate that it hadn't proved possible to find a way around this technicality, because if Rotardier *had* been guilty, he would not have been free to kill again. This highlights the fact that miscarriages of justice work both ways – by resulting in conviction of the innocent, as well as failure to convict the guilty and protect potential future victims.

Forging someone else's handwriting for criminal purposes is common. The analysis and comparison of handwriting form part of the work of the forensic questioned documents expert. (This type of handwriting analysis is quite different from the pseudo-science graphology, which claims to be able to divine essential traits of a writer's personality.) As well as examining a questioned document visually, including with a microscope, expert forensic scientists can use a range of different light sources to detect additions, obliterations and alterations that will not be visible under ordinary white light.

Every character of the alphabet – both capitals and lower case – and all numerals can be formed in a number of different ways. When handwriting is taught in schools, students follow the example of their teacher and, to begin with, the writing of all the students in a class will be similar. But as it develops over time, and specific features are added by each student with practice, the writing becomes more individual and fixed by early adulthood. From then on, it will generally remain much the same, although it can undergo further developmental changes and be affected by factors such as illness, alcohol, drugs and, ultimately, old age. For these reasons, it is best when comparing suspect and known writings that they relate whenever possible to the same era.

It is due to the particular combination of specific forms of each of the characters, both on their own and combined together in the writing, that no two people will produce exactly the same form of writing. Because there will also be a natural range of variation in any one person's writing, any sample of known writing needs to be sufficiently extensive to capture that range. Therefore, the smaller the amount of writing in a sample, the less confident a handwriting expert is likely to be about its potential provenance.

The fact that handwriting becomes a subconscious process means that we only have to think about *what* we are writing, not *how* we are writing it. Indeed, if we do stop to think about how we are doing it, our writing becomes less fluent and the characters much less consistent. This means that samples produced specifically for the purpose of comparison – known as specimen writings – are not as reliable as those produced naturally.

For these reasons, forgery involving someone trying to simulate someone else's writing always ends up being a compromise between fluency and accuracy, as the writer tries to suppress their own writing style and imitate the other person's. While they may achieve a superficially similar overall look to their simulation, it is unlikely to stand the test in terms of detail; and the longer the sample of handwriting, the more obvious this will be. Tell-tale signs of copying include hesitations and pen lifts in unexpected places, differences in the fluency and quality of the writing, and the use of odd forms of individual characters.

Sometimes, of course, people do the precise opposite of forging when they try to disguise their own handwriting for reasons such as signing an agreement that they do not want to be held to in the future. This will result in the introduction of inconsistencies such as variation in slope, unusual ways of constructing individual characters, and the addition of loops and other flourishes.

General features that are of particular interest to handwriting experts include the overall style of the writing, and the size, slope, relative proportions and quality of the component characters. More detailed features relate to the way the pen is moved across the paper to create the characters and, in cursive writing, to join them together, which can sometimes indicate if the writer is left-handed or right-handed.

Conclusions about whether someone has authored a particular piece of writing are based on consideration of the numbers and types of similarities and any differences between the suspected and known writings. Substantial similarities will strengthen evidence of common authorship. But just a single fundamental difference will usually indicate that the suspect piece was written by someone else.

Use of language and patterns of word usage, known as forensic linguistics, can also be important in comparisons of written passages, and there are now computer programs that can assist with this aspect, as well as in detecting plagiarism. Also of potential significance are the ink used and the general appearance and composition of the paper on which the piece has been written.

After gaining a doctorate in chemistry at King's College London in the early 1930s, Dr Julius Grant started work as a scientist in the paper industry. In 1983, he was working in London at a company called Hehner & Cox – which he later owned – when he was asked by the then owner of *The Sunday Times*, Rupert Murdoch, to examine some diaries that were purported to have been written by Adolf Hitler prior to the Second World War.

Using a needle to remove fibres from the dampened edges of some of the pages, Grant examined them under a microscope. What he found was that the paper was made of recycled material comprised of wood pulp from mostly coniferous trees and bleached by techniques that had not been available at the time of Hitler's death in the 1940s. So, despite having been thought to be genuine by authoritative figures that included the historian Hugh Trevor-Roper, the 'Hitler diaries' were finally judged to be forgeries, for which forger Konrad Kujau subsequently served a prison sentence.

Signatures are a special form of writing in that they may look like the normal handwriting of the person to whom they relate, or may be so highly stylised that it is not possible to make out the name at all. When forgery is suspected – by either copying or tracing – the handwriting expert will look at the same sorts of features as in general writings. When the signatures are not complex, errors in construction are likely to be minor and not obvious. So fluency becomes more important – for example, variation in the pressure of the ink line, unexpected hesitations or pen lifts, and the direction in which the stroke is written.

Guided-hand signatures, such as those written by someone who is elderly or infirm and needs some assistance, are a tricky area for document examiners. This is because they are likely to contain a mixture of characteristics from the signatory and the person assisting them. In these circumstances, and particularly when the assistant's characteristics predominate, questions may be asked about the influence the assistant may have had over the signatory and about their own intent in relation to the signing.

A questioned document is anything, written or printed, that might be used in an investigation and/or as evidence in court, and therefore the authenticity of which needs to be verified. Examples include cheques, wills, title deeds, birth and marriage certificates, passports, invoices, criminal confessions, suicide and ransom notes, letters – handwritten, typed, printed, photocopied and computer generated – and counterfeit money. Legal documents – i.e. documents that may be used in legal proceedings of one sort or another – can be involved in civil disputes and criminal prosecutions.

Counterfeit documents can be linked to a specific computer printer or photocopier. Shredded, torn, burnt or otherwise damaged documents can be reconstructed. In the past, typewritten documents were a rich source of evidence, as small, consistent defects within particular characters and in their alignment could provide very good links with the specific typewriters they had been produced on. The inked ribbons against which the letters were struck to leave their impressions on the paper, as well as the carbon sheets that were used to make copies, would also hold clues about what had been typed with them. Then there are other types of evidence, such as fingerprints and DNA from people who have touched the paper, and other traces that may have dropped on to it from them or their environment.

Sometimes – although not as often in real life as some TV shows would have us believe – people use letters cut out of a newspaper or magazine to create their messages, as happened in the case involving the Reverend Janet Magee.

Reverend Magee was the Methodist minister of a church in Lincolnshire when she made several reports to the police over a period of about three years claiming to have received obscene hate mail and unpleasant telephone calls, as well as a dead hedgehog and excrement in the post. Similar hate mail had also been received by other members of her congregation, and at one point during the investigation, police arrested a Methodist steward, but then released him without charge.

The police eventually began to suspect that Janet Magee herself might have been responsible for the hate mail and for the campaign of which she claimed to be the subject. After extensive enquiries and the installation of a CCTV camera without her knowledge, she was arrested and charged with attempting to pervert the course of justice.

The evidence in the case included the discovery in Magee's house of pieces of newspaper with letters cut out of them. These formed jigsaw fits with a number of the letters in four separate examples of the hate mail that began with the words: 'are there only two people', 'they won't see her', 'dead like you'll be soon' and 'you ****ing bitch'.

At her trial in October 2008, the Reverend Janet Magee was found guilty of perverting the course of justice – by what the judge described as making false claims 'to attract sympathy or attention' – and was given a six-month suspended sentence.

When someone writes on a piece of paper that has other pages underneath it – in a notepad, for example, or on one of several pages of a document – the writing creates indentations on the page (or pages) beneath. These indentations can be enhanced and made legible by a highly sensitive technique known as electrostatic detection analysis (ESDA).

The ESDA technique involves using suction to draw down the questioned document together with a length of clingfilm on top of it on to the brass grid of a vacuum box, then passing an electrostatic charge through the paper. The charge concentrates in the indentations, which can then be visualised by the application of negatively charged toner, which collects in them.

Sometimes, the indentations detected might be evidence that a confession has been tampered with after it was written or signed. When found on something like a ransom note or other anonymous letter, they can also provide information about the sender that might lead to the identification of a suspect. When used to prove that confessions and witness statements have been altered, ESDA has played a part in the overturning of numerous convictions, including those of the 'Birmingham Six'.

In 1975, six IRA suspects were imprisoned after being found guilty of planting bombs in two pubs in Birmingham that caused the deaths of twenty-one people and injuries to many more. When their case went to appeal for a second time in 1991, it was revealed that members of the West Midlands Serious Crime Squad, who had interrogated the suspects after their arrests and had obtained confessions from four of the six men, had beaten and tortured them. What the ESDA evidence also showed, by revealing indentations on the pages in the police officers' notebooks, was that they had written (and rewritten) false accounts of the interrogations. As a result, the convictions of all six of the men were quashed by the Court of

Appeal and they were subsequently awarded substantial sums of money in compensation.

The term forensic linguistics was first used in the late 1960s by the Swedish linguistics expert Jan Svartvik in relation to a case involving a man called Timothy Evans. Evans had been found guilty of murdering his wife and daughter. But when Svartvik compared the grammatical style of parts of the transcript of his interview with the rest of the recording, he found significant discrepancies that led to Evans being officially pardoned – although, unfortunately, he had been hanged some twenty years previously.

In civil cases, it may be possible for a forensic linguist to ascertain whether a particular book or other work of literature was actually written by the supposed author. In criminal cases, forensic linguistics can also be used to examine the spelling, punctuation, use of words and construction of sentences in documents such as suicide and ransom notes. And it can prove useful in analysing correspondence intended to make the recipient believe a murder victim is still alive.

I remember a case I once investigated in Oxford where a young woman living in student-type accommodation had suddenly gone missing. Her disappearance apparently seemed very out of character but, shortly afterwards, her friends received a postcard from her, posted in France, which suggested that she might be all right. Some days later, her body was found underneath her own bed – where it had obviously been all the time. After the investigation became focused on the handwriting and turn of phrase on the postcard, it wasn't long before the young woman's boyfriend was identified as the author, and he was subsequently convicted of her murder.

In spoken language, it is relevant features in accent, dialect, use and pronunciation of certain words, the pitch and tone of the voice, and the speed of articulation that can help to identify who called the emergency services or left the message on a mobile phone. The fastest growing area of forensic linguistics currently, however, relates to text messages and questions of authorship of these, and large reference databases are being created to assist with this.

Sometimes, speech and audio experts assist the police in setting up voice identification parades for witnesses, or provide a 'speaker profile' that the police can then use in their attempts to identify an offender. Analysis of a voice recording can indicate possible editing or tampering with it. Enhancement of a recording can ensure the fullest transcription of what has been said, and may enable more effective interviewing of witnesses and evaluation of their statements and answers to questions.

Another striking example of the use of speech and audio analysis was in the investigation of a series of murders that were committed by the man who became known as 'the Yorkshire Ripper'.

Peter Sutcliffe's criminal activity could have started as early as 1969, and he killed his last victim in November 1980. Between March 1978 and June 1979, the police received three anonymous letters (one via the *Daily Mail* newspaper) and a tape recording from someone who claimed to be responsible for the attacks and who signed himself 'Jack the Ripper'. The letters and tape were postmarked Sunderland, and the message on the tape had been spoken by someone with a Sunderland accent, who became known in the media as 'Wearside Jack'. But despite the fact that two eminent forensic speech experts – Stanley Ellis and Jack Windsor Lewis – said that they believed the letters and tape were a hoax, the police ignored them. So the speech-related information completely hijacked the investigation, and it was several months before it got back on a more useful track.

The letters and tape were finally confirmed as a hoax when Peter Sutcliffe was identified as the murderer of thirteen women following his apprehension by two sharp-eyed young police officers. The officers were actually investigating some false number plates on a car occupied by Sutcliffe and a prostitute when they heard a thud on the ground while Sutcliffe was relieving himself before being taken to the police station for questioning. When they returned later to check out what might have caused the sound, they discovered a hammer – of the kind the Yorkshire Ripper was known to use to incapacitate his victims before mutilating their bodies.

Years later, my colleague Chris Gregg – who was Head of West Yorkshire CID at the time – managed to track down the hoaxer, and 'Wearside Jack' turned out to be a man from Sunderland called John Humble.

Identifying Humble had been far from straightforward, as the hoax letters and their envelopes had long since been destroyed in extensive testing for fingerprints. But with characteristically dogged determination, Chris went back to the FSS laboratory at Wetherby that had conducted some of the original work to check that they really didn't have anything else that might conceivably be useful. And he was as surprised as anyone when, after initial denials, they finally found and presented him with a tiny strip of gummed envelope flap, perfectly preserved between two glass microscope slides, which had come from one of the letters.

When tested, the strip produced a full DNA profile, which matched the profile on the National DNA Database from John Humble. (Humble's sample had been added to the database some five years previously in relation to an unconnected minor crime.)

Chris then invited Professor Peter French, the UK's pre-eminent speech and audio analysis expert, to compare the original recording from the hoaxer – made twenty-six years earlier – and recordings of Humble's voice in the recent police interviews and when he read a transcription of the hoaxer's tape recording.

Humble was apparently alcoholic and a heavy smoker, and

Peter wondered whether, over the years, this might have altered his voice. But the comparison showed such a high degree of correspondence between the two voices that he concluded there was only the remotest chance that the recording had been made by anyone else. In fact, Chris said his blood had run cold when he heard Humble read out the transcript, so accurately did it mirror the original recording.

In 2006, John Humble was sentenced to eight years in prison for perverting the cause of justice.

It isn't just speech that forensic speech and audio experts analyse. It can be other sounds on recordings that can be critical to an investigation, such as distinguishing between a gunshot and the sound of a car door slamming, and precisely when it happened. In one example from another of Peter French's cases, it was coughing that was the issue.

It was during a 2001 recording of the popular television show *Who Wants to Be a Millionaire?* that suspicions were raised among programme staff due to the unusual playing style of one of the contestants and the amount of coughing that was going on in the studio. The contestant was a British Army major called Charles Ingram, and it turned out that Ingram, another contestant called Tecwen Whittock, and Ingram's wife, Diana, had a strategy. After having been asked a question, Ingram would repeat each of the possible answers out loud while Whittock, who was also in the studio, guided him to the right one by coughing at the appropriate moment.

The police identified nineteen specific coughs that they believed were 'prompting coughs'. Then they asked Peter to locate the cougher in the audience of 260 people through analysis of recordings from twenty-one different microphones positioned in various sites in what was a round auditorium. Eight of these microphones were in fixed positions above the audience. The remaining thirteen were radio microphones on the host of the show; on Ingram, as the hot-seat contestant; on his wife, as accompanying partner; and on the other potential contestants for the hot seat – including Tecwen Whittock.

In the end, by analysing outputs from each of the microphones – taking into account complications from routing and mixing of the microphone outputs – Peter managed to identify Whittock as the source of the coughing. He also showed how the cougher had been able to utilise useful information from the quiet discussion within the potential hot-seat contestant group about the answers.

Charles and Diana Ingram and Tecwen Whittock were ultimately convicted of attempting to defraud the programme of the £1m prize. The Ingrams were sentenced to eighteen months in prison and Whittock to twelve months, all suspended for two years. They were each also fined a substantial amount of money.

This chapter provides a good illustration of the breadth of expertise that is involved in everyday forensic science. Just forgery and fraud alone involve all aspects of documents – from handwriting and phraseology to paper and printers – and all the types of traces that can be associated with them, including personal traces such as fingerprints and DNA. In addition, they involve all aspects of people's voices, from accent, dialect and use of certain words, to the pitch and tone of the voice and speed of articulation, as well as the technology that captures and analyses these. Multiply all of that many times over, and include some more esoteric types of forensic expertise, and you have the fascinating world of forensic science. No wonder the last forty-seven years of my career have gone by so quickly!

16

Presenting evidence in court

There are three main – and strongly interlinked – aspects to a forensic scientist's job. The first is attending scenes of some of the more serious crimes as part of the Senior Investigating Officer's (SIO's) team of crime scene investigators. This involves helping to establish the detail of what is likely to have taken place there, and advising about which items and samples it might be best to collect – and the most effective way of doing this – to help determine who might have been responsible. The second is all the laboratory work that ensues, and the examination and analysis of other items and samples from any suspects or anyone else who might conceivably have played a part in the crime. Finally, there is the presentation to the court of the results of all the testing, and of the conclusions it has been possible to draw from it that might help judge and jury to decide on the probable (beyond reasonable doubt in criminal cases) innocence or guilt of the defendants.

All three of those aspects are important in relation to any type of crime, and particularly when someone might be rightly or wrongly deprived of their liberty based at least partly on the scientific evidence itself and on how comprehensive and understandable it is when presented in court. So it can be a bit nerve-racking being an expert witness in a courtroom, sometimes on a case that you may have worked on many months earlier. And I can remember, whenever I gave evidence at the

Old Bailey in London, being inspired and encouraged by the quote relating to the social reformer Elizabeth Fry that was engraved under her statue there:

> *One who never turned her* back,*
> *But marched breast forward,*
> *Never doubted clouds would break,*
> *Never dreamed, though right were worsted, wrong would*
>   *triumph,*
> *Held we fall to rise,*
> *Are baffled to fight better,*
> *Sleep to wake.*

Perhaps the most important aspect of presenting forensic evidence in court is ensuring that the jurors understand both the facts and the contextual implications of what you're saying. This means that the lawyers have to understand it first, so that they can ask the right questions to draw out its strengths and weaknesses – depending on whether they are acting for the prosecution or defence in the case. To help with this, scientists usually have to write formal statements of evidence. These statements may be read out in the absence of the scientist, or the scientist may be asked to give evidence in person, which enables them to provide more detail, if required, and also allows them to be cross-examined to test any suspected areas of weakness in their evidence. To assist with this, other scientists may be invited to be present in court when the evidence is being given, so that they can suggest lines of questioning that may be helpful to those representing the other side of the case. These scientists may

* To make it applicable to Elizabeth Fry, the word 'his' was changed to 'her' in this quote from a poem by Robert Browning entitled 'Epilogue' from the collection of his poems *Asolando*.

even go so far as predicting the answers the scientist will give to a specific line of questioning.

I remember being asked to attend court to help with the questioning of an FSS scientist who I thought had gone way over the top in expressing his opinion about a case. When he remained resolute, I took the most unusual step of approaching a senior manager to suggest that it might be a good idea to conduct a general review of the scientist's work. I think this must have been done, because shortly afterwards he was removed from his court reporting duties and set on something else.

A scientist will normally give evidence for one side *or* the other in a criminal case. But in one extraordinary instance that occurred during the trial of the Preddie brothers, who were accused of killing ten-year-old Damilola Taylor in London in November 2000 (see Chapter 8), one scientist provided advice for both prosecution *and* defence. The scientist in question worked for the FSS, which had been responsible for some of the initial work on the case, including the examination of a pair of trainers from one of the brothers. No blood had been detected on the trainers, but when we re-examined them some years later, we found a 9-mm bloodstain on the back of the heel of the right shoe, which contained DNA that matched Damilola's.

During the second trial in 2006, the FSS scientist first advised the prosecution about the original investigation. Then he suggested, for the defence, that the blood on the trainer had not been present when the shoe was first examined, and therefore must have resulted from some type of contamination event that had occurred subsequently. It was the first – and only – time we had ever come across a scientist advising both sides in a case in this way. Fortunately, we were able to point to a Polaroid photograph in the case notes, which had been made at the time of the first (FSS) examination and showed that the bloodstain *was* in place at that time. So it was obvious that it had just been missed. But it was an example of the fact that you have to be ready for anything and able to work out how to deal with whatever is thrown at you so that the court can have confidence in what you're saying.

Jury members deserve the greatest respect for the extremely difficult job they have to do. As part of that job, they are expected to absorb and understand all the different kinds of evidence with which they are often presented. Some of this evidence – such as that related to forensic science – can include large amounts of technical detail, which, depending on the skill of the scientist reporting it, can be very dry. Indeed, learning to 'read' a jury in terms of being able to assess their level of engagement with what you are telling them is a core skill that all reporting forensic scientists have to master. Of course, when you realise that you *are* losing the attention of jurors, you need to be able to do something about it.

Signs that attention may be wandering are fairly easy to detect. For example, jurors' eyes may glaze over, or even – so I've heard – people may actually fall asleep. So how do you make your evidence more accessible without losing any of its precision or accuracy? Also, how do you convince the jury that, despite what the opposing counsel might suggest in order to press their side of the case, you have no axe to grind, are not yourself on any 'side' at all, and your sole concern is to present the scientific facts of the forensic evidence honestly and dispassionately?

A good start is to use everyday terms that jury members – and, indeed, judges and barristers, who may have little or no scientific knowledge – can relate to. This may include describing amounts in teaspoonfuls rather than grammes, and areas as the size of a little fingernail or the top of a pinhead, for example. It may also be useful to use analogies that involve the sorts of experiences jurors will be familiar with in their everyday lives, such as the difficulty of cleaning up blood after a nosebleed, when there will always be some specks of it left somewhere. And it is a good idea to be as succinct as possible and avoid giving overly long answers. What might help in this respect is to bear in mind that no one is there for a lecture, however fascinating a particular scientific detail might be to the forensic scientist involved!

Sometimes, opposing counsel might try to discredit any evidence that doesn't suit their case by accusing the witness of incompetence or bias. Occasionally their cross-examination can be quite aggressive. But however insulting and wide of the mark their accusations might be, it is important to remain calm. And that's easier to do when you realise that jurors are usually able to see through such tactics and focus on the evidence that is being presented.

When employed for the defence, I would sometimes sit in court and listen to the evidence being given by the forensic scientist employed for the prosecution, so that I could then advise the defence team about its strengths and weaknesses. Once when I was doing this, the defence barrister was giving the prosecution's forensic scientist a particularly difficult time – not, on this occasion, in relation to any advice I had given. Afterwards, the forensic scientist told me that as she came down from the witness box and was walking past the end of the jury bench, one of the jurors whispered some words of support and encouragement to her, along the lines of 'Well done, Doc,' which rather indicated that he been able to see through the courtroom theatrics.

Waiting to give evidence in court can be quite tiring. I think it's because you never know exactly when you're going to be called to the witness stand. And the court doesn't know either, as it can be difficult to predict how long it is going to take to hear the other evidence that has to be heard before you. So you often have to remain in a state of extreme preparedness for several hours – sometimes, in the worst cases, over a period of a couple of days or more.

You also have to be very careful not to talk to anyone else who might be involved in some other role in the case and who may have an ulterior motive for engaging you in conversation. This was brought home to me on one occasion when a man who had been talking to the solicitor who had instructed me offered me a cup of coffee while I was waiting to give my evidence. Assuming him to be the solicitor's clerk, I agreed. But then I quickly had to make my excuses and leave after he set the coffee down in front of me and it became clear that he was actually the defendant!

Sometimes, in the early days, a barrister working on what was ostensibly 'the same side' of the case would stick to the old-fashioned ways and only talk to me through the solicitor, rather than directly. Perhaps it was with some idea of not risking being thought to be coaching a witness. But I always found this rather disconcerting. Nowadays, it is also more usual for scientists on both sides to be asked to get together to see to what extent they can agree before the court session, or even during it if there's something that someone wants to clarify. This ensures that the court then deals only with matters in dispute between them.

Another aspect of being a witness in court is the wearing of sober clothing. Indeed, I have known of solicitors and forensic colleagues who have been criticised in court for wearing articles of clothing that were deemed to be inappropriate – for example, a 'loud' tie in one case and a colourful blouse in another.

You have to be prepared for almost anything when entering a courtroom as an expert witness and take your time when formulating your answers to specific questions. Risking irritating the other side is nothing compared with the complications that can arise from responding too hastily or providing an ill-considered answer.

17

Knots, ropes and cordage

Knots, ropes and cordage can play a critical role in various types of cases dealt with by forensic scientists. One example of a case in which untying a knot at the scene was to prove a complicating factor in a forensic investigation involved the death of Italian banker Roberto Calvi.

The body of 62-year-old Calvi was found hanging from scaffolding under Blackfriars Bridge in London early one morning in June 1982. After untying the rope from around his neck, officers from Thames River Police transported his body by boat to Waterloo Police Pier.

There were lumps of concrete and half-bricks in the pockets of Calvi's jacket, as well as in the pockets and inside the crotch of his trousers. But no injuries or any other marks were found on his body during the post-mortem examination to indicate that he had been subjected to any kind of physical force. The autopsy report stated the cause of death to be asphyxiation due to hanging, and an inquest that was subsequently held in London recorded a verdict of suicide.

Prior to his arrival in London and a few days before his death, Banco Ambrosiano – of which Calvi was chairman and which had close links to the Vatican – collapsed amid allegations of illegal transactions. Calvi was also apparently a member of an illegal Masonic lodge that was known as *i fratineri*, which translates – interestingly, in view of where he was found – as 'the black friars'. However, it was his family's belief that committing suicide was an unimaginable step for someone who was as devout a Catholic as he had been that led to a second inquest being held a year later, at which an open verdict was returned.

Convinced that Calvi had been murdered, his family secured the services of a private investigation company, and some ten years after his death, I became involved in the case.

As well as examining the foreshore of the River Thames under and around Blackfriars Bridge, I conducted a series of experiments involving some of Calvi's other clothing – which was sent from Italy for the purpose – and parts of the original scaffolding. These experiments were designed to discover which of four possible routes he was most likely to have taken to end up on the scaffolding where he was found. Two of those routes would have involved murder, and two of them suicide. And as my investigation proceeded, it became obvious that he must have been murdered.

In 2003, after both the Italian and British authorities had accepted this conclusion, five suspects were charged with Roberto Calvi's murder, but subsequently acquitted in the Italian courts due to lack of evidence.

It might seem that untying the knot in the rope around the dead man's neck had been a fairly insignificant action. In fact though, the knot could have contained traces trapped between the strands of the rope that were related to where it had come from and the person who had tied it. Depending on the circumstances, such traces – which would have been compromised or lost when the knot was untied instead of being cut – can include textile fibres, hairs, paint flakes, soil particles, glass fragments, bits of wood and vegetation, and DNA, although DNA profiling wasn't available at the time of Calvi's death.

There are various principles governing the treatment of knotted ropes or cords at a crime scene, which are designed to preserve as much evidence as possible. The first of these – as in the Calvi case – is never to untie a knot, but instead to cut the rope to one side of it. Adhesive tape is wrapped around the rope before a cut is made in the middle of it, thus securing each of the cut ends so that they don't unravel, and 'trapping' any tiny particles of potential evidence that may be present. The end of the rope that was originally attached to the side of the knot is labelled, so that the knotted rope can be reconstructed back at the laboratory.

Reconstructions are never a completely accurate reflection of the original, so another principle is to make as few cuts as possible. The usual precautions required for any exhibit that is going to be examined also apply, such as making sure that all potential evidential traces have been removed from the rope before trying to work out what type of knot (or knots) has been tied in it.

Most people without any specialised knowledge of tying knots tend to use overhand knots repeatedly. Although this can result in quite complicated-looking structures, their construction soon becomes obvious when they are teased apart. Two identical overhand knots tied one on top of the other – e.g. right over left followed by right over left – will result in a granny knot. As this is fairly insecure, a third overhand knot is usually added. But if the second overhand knot is opposed to the first one – i.e. right over left followed by left over right, or vice versa – this will result in a reef knot, which is more secure.

There are very few forensic knot experts, so identifying anything other than the simplest knots can be problematic. When it *is* possible, however, the identification of a specific type of knot can provide a clue to the sort of person who might have tied it, in terms of their occupation, at least. This is because, in many industries, specific methods of knotting ropes and cords have been developed to provide the functionality required. Anyone who has ever watched a fisherman mending nets, or a weaver knotting yarn, or a mountaineer preparing to abseil down a sheer rockface, will appreciate the skill involved and the reliance they place on their own knotting abilities, particularly in situations in which their lives, quite literally, depend on them.

As Geoffrey Budworth, one of the rare species of forensic knot experts, once observed, what complicates matters is that the same knot can be called different things in different industries. For example, the miller's knot that is used to close a sack of grain, the picket-line hitch used to tether horses, and the ground-line hitch that secures deep-sea fishing nets are all the same knots. Conversely, any one of the dozen or so different knots used to secure parcels is likely to be referred to as the packer's knot. Another confounding factor is that some knots can be capsized (i.e. have their structure altered depending on how they have been handled) into others – the reef knot pulls over into a lark's head, for example, and the granny knot into two half hitches.

So how does one establish which type of knot one is dealing with? To help answer this question, Budworth developed a classification system based on the number of crossing points in the knot, i.e. where one part of the rope or cord crosses another part. In order to determine this, the knot must be carefully teased loose and spread out flat. Simple as that may sound, it can actually prove quite tricky, as extra crossing points can be inadvertently created during the process as the result of accidental rearrangements of the knot.

Despite these complications, Budworth described as many as 135 different knots with anything between one and twenty-four crossing points. (For anyone who is a knot enthusiast and who hasn't just learned more about knots than they ever wanted to know, *The Ashley Book of Knots* – which has been reprinted numerous times since its publication in 1944, with amendments by Budworth himself in 1993 – includes 7,000 drawings representing more than 3,800 different knots.)

According to Budworth, as well as possibly providing information about the employment of the person who tied a particular knot, or what hobbies they might have, the way a knot is tied can also indicate whether the person who tied it is likely to be short or tall. Sometimes, what it can certainly indicate in the case of someone who has been tied up is whether the knot was self-tied or tied by someone else – which was another reason why it was a mistake for the police to have untied the knot in the case of Roberto Calvi described above.

Another potential source of useful forensic evidence in cases involving knots and rope is the rope itself, which comes in a wide variety of types. Finding that a length of rope that has been used to bind the hands and/or feet of a victim matches a length of rope found in a suspect's car, for example, can be extremely important in establishing a link between suspect and victim. Proving such a 'match' requires an understanding of the construction and composition of rope.

When a match between two ropes is established, the next step for the forensic scientist is to try to identify the manufacturer, how much of the rope was made, and where it was distributed. The reason why this information is important is because knowing how commonly a particular rope might be encountered in a specific locality can either strengthen or weaken the evidence provided to the case by the match that has been made.

One case in which rope comprised part of the forensic investigation involved the brutal murder in February 1990 of an eminent dermatologist called Dr David Birkett. After being attacked in the hallway of his house in Middlesbrough, Dr Birkett was struck repeatedly on the head with a hammer wrapped in a plastic carrier bag. His body was then dragged into the study, where it was found by his daughter.

When a forensic scientist from the FSS laboratory at Wetherby visited the scene, he described the nature and distribution of bloodstaining in the house and on a carrier bag that had been left behind there. He also recorded the presence of two lengths of green-and-black cord close to the victim's body. Although it wasn't possible to say what purpose, if any, the cord had been used for, he suggested that it could have been looped over Dr Birkett's arms and used to drag his body from the hall into the study.

It was a right-hand thumbprint on the carrier bag that led police some weeks later to Reginald Wilson, who denied ever having been in the house, let alone having killed the victim there. During their investigations, however, the police noticed some green-and-black cord on a fence post in Wilson's back garden. When the forensic scientist compared this with the cord at the murder scene, he found that it matched in terms of its construction, the appearance of the component parts, and the way in which the strands of green and black fibres had been interwoven to form the outer sheath.

The forensic scientist also examined samples of the green, black and colourless nylon fibres, by comparing them under the microscope and analysing their chemical composition using infra-red spectroscopy (FTIR). He then used microspectrophotometry (MSP) to examine the colour of the green fibres, and thin-layer chromatography to analyse their dyestuff.

When I looked at the cords myself and checked samples of the fibres from them, I agreed with what had been said about them. But how strong a link they provided with Wilson was another matter. One of the limiting factors in this respect was that having traced the manufacturer of the cord, we discovered that it was incorporated in a particular make of dog lead, and possibly in other products too.

More than a million of the dog leads were produced every year, about 300,000 of which were imported into the UK, and 4,000 were sold in the area local to where the crime had been committed. Not all of the leads were green and black – they also came in four other colours, and in two different lengths. Also, no comparison had been made between the cord that featured in the case and a sample dog lead, which would have been important to be able to confirm its relative commonness.

What it *was* possible to say, however, was that the cord appeared to be relatively unusual. Combined with other evidence, notably the thumbprint that had been found on the carrier bag, this provided a stronger link with the suspect than there might otherwise have been. And in 1991, Reginald Wilson was convicted of the apparently random murder of Dr David Birkett and sentenced to thirty years in prison.

Just like every other type of forensic evidence, rope is never just 'any old rope'. It has its own distinguishing features relating to what it's made from and how these constituents have been woven or twisted together. It also provides the means for trapping tiny traces that can indicate what it might have been used for previously, and who might have used it in connection with the crime that is being investigated. This is especially true if knots have been tied in the rope – as long as these are not untied before a forensic scientist can get their hands on it.

18

Never assume

One of the cardinal rules of forensic investigation – and probably of anything else that involves human behaviour – is never to make assumptions. It was something I learned quite quickly after I started working at the FSS laboratory in Harrogate in 1974, and it has been well illustrated by many of the cases I've worked on since then.

One of those cases – which occurred in 1982, after I had moved to the FSS lab at Aldermaston in Berkshire – involved the discovery of the body of an elderly woman on a bed in a bungalow that had been wrecked by fire.

Smoking in bed has been the cause of many fires in people's homes, and when we were called in by the Hampshire Constabulary, it was simply being treated as a case of suspicious death. So while my fire-expert colleague looked for evidence to establish where, when and how the fire had started and how long it had been burning, I searched for any biological evidence that might indicate whether or not the woman's death had been accidental.

Although the bed did turn out to be the seat of the fire, the falling-asleep-while-smoking theory was blown apart when I discovered traces of blood. These included blood spatter on the bedding and adjacent wall, and some blood and head hair on a glass vase, which was subsequently found to match an injury the pathologist noted on the dead woman's head.

One of the odd, and intriguing, things I and my colleague noticed in that particular case was the presence of numerous balls of newspaper, which were found, mostly unburnt, under a sofa and armchair in the bungalow. Once it had been established that the fire was probably not accidental and the woman had been murdered, the most logical explanation seemed to be that the balls of newspaper had been placed there by whoever had set the fire, with the intention of assisting the spread of the flames.

Sometimes though, what seems to be the most logical explanation isn't the right one. And in this case, according to what a neighbour told the police, it turned out that the dead woman had a habit of rolling up sheets of newspaper and stuffing them under the furniture – for reasons I don't think anyone ever understood. So although they might have played a role in assisting the spread of the fire, it would have been wrong to have assumed that they had necessarily been put there with that intention.

When investigating any crime scene, it is important to be able to mull over what one has seen, and to go back and check if certain things seem odd or out of place, especially if there was no obvious explanation for them. One example of something that seemed at first to have no obvious explanation was the discovery of DNA that appeared to be from the daughter of two murder victims on a pair of shorts that were thought to belong to their suspected killer.

It was 2006 and John Cooper was already serving a prison sentence for burglary and violent armed robbery when we were asked by Detective Superintendent Steve Wilkins to look into the cold-case murders of Gwenda and Peter Dixon. The couple, who lived in Oxfordshire, were on holiday alone when they were killed on the Pembrokeshire Coastal Path in Wales in June 1989. So there was no reason why their daughter, Julie, would ever have come into contact with their killer, and, at first, it looked as though we might have got it wrong.

That's certainly what the police and, particularly, the lawyers assumed when they told us that the suggestion that Julie's DNA might be on Cooper's shorts was 'preposterous' and we needed to go away and think again. But when we did as they asked – and involved a specialist DNA statistician – the evidence of a link with Julie only became stronger. So then we did what we always do in circumstances like that: we went back to the crime scene to see if there was anything there that might explain what we had found.

When the Dixons' bodies were discovered, a week after they went missing on the last day of the holiday they had spent at a nearby campsite, they were partially hidden by branches on a strip of land to one side of the coastal path adjacent to a cliff. Gwenda had been sexually assaulted and shot twice at close range. Peter had been shot three times, also at close range, and his hands were tied behind his back. What was clear from the original photographs taken of the scene was that whoever murdered them had turned out their rucksacks and scattered the contents on the ground.

Among the scattered items in the photographs was some spare clothing, including a pair of shorts. So, what if their murderer, splashed and smeared with their blood as he was very likely to have been, simply exchanged the shorts he was wearing for a pair of theirs – which might have had a tiny amount of their daughter's DNA on them?

Of particular interest was the fact that the hems of a pair of shorts seized from Cooper's house had been taken up since manufacture. That could account for them being slightly shorter than those worn by a man who was seen by a witness to be acting suspiciously at around the time the Dixons disappeared, and whose likeness was captured in a Photofit picture. And indeed, when the hems of the seized shorts were unpicked, the DNA that could have come from Julie Dixon was found inside one of them, which indicated that it had been deposited when the shorts were longer.

In the end, far from detracting from the evidence we already had to link the shorts worn by Cooper with the murdered couple – as the police and lawyers had assumed it would – the DNA evidence linking them to the Dixons' daughter positively enhanced it.

Sometimes, an unexpected death is too readily assumed to be a tragic accident or suicide, or a double death might be concluded to be a murder/suicide. For instance, after the bodies of brother and sister Richard and Helen Thomas were found when firefighters attended a fire at their manor house near Milford Haven in Wales in 1985, it was assumed that Richard Thomas had committed suicide after killing his sister. It wasn't until we became involved in the cold-case investigation of the murders of Gwenda and Peter Dixon that we looked again at that case too, and were able to establish that the Thomases had also been killed by John Cooper.

What the investigation into the Pembrokeshire Coastal Path murders of the Dixons – and the racially motivated killing in London of Stephen Lawrence in 1993 – also illustrated is that one should never assume the only evidence that really matters is DNA. With its powerful statistics, DNA is likely to be one form of evidence that, ideally, you'd like to end up with. But you might have to start somewhere else first, as my colleagues and I did in both of those cases.

Another case involving a death that was assumed to be accidental – despite the rather bizarre circumstances – was that of Florence Evans. Florence was in her seventies when her body was found, lying fully clothed in a bath of cold water, in her home in Pembrokeshire. It was shortly after the discovery of the bodies of the Dixons on the Pembroke Coastal Path in 1989. And it was John Cooper himself who mentioned

Florence Evans to the police during the investigation into the Dixons' deaths.

According to Florence's family, her house keys had gone missing a few days before she died. There were other aspects of her death that they found perplexing too, including the fact that the water in the bath was cold and she hadn't lit the fire in the kitchen that would have heated it. Also, it turned out later that Cooper and his wife used to visit Florence at her home, where Cooper would sometimes do odd jobs for her. But an inquest recorded a verdict of accidental death, and Dyfed-Powys Police have said that they currently have no plans to re-investigate the case.

Among other cases in which it seems that assumptions may have been made that would perhaps benefit from reconsidering are the deaths of Megan and Harry Tooze in their isolated farmhouse at Llanharry near Bridgend in 1993, as described in Chapter 26.

What these cases illustrate is that it is never safe to assume that just because nobody has found any evidence yet, it isn't there. You might just have to look harder, or more imaginatively, or in different places. Because one of the things I've learned during my career as a forensic scientist is that every contact really does leave a trace. Also, from the point of view of the perpetrators of crime, never assume that if you haven't been caught by now, you never will be.

19

Fetishes

Working as a forensic scientist obviously gives you a broader than normal insight into some of the things human beings are capable of doing. Sometimes, people's actions are at least understandable – if not excusable – such as theft and crimes of passion committed in the heat of the moment. But sometimes they are just plain odd – on occasion, odd enough to have brought me and my fellow scientists up short. Perhaps the most bizarre in my own experience involved a man who had come to the attention of the police after he had opened his front door to an Avon Lady while wearing a brassiere over his shirt.

The police probably wouldn't normally have thought much more about it. But the incident occurred in West Yorkshire at the time when they were desperately hunting the Yorkshire Ripper, and when anything out of the ordinary was going to attract their attention. So they arranged for us to examine the house where the man lived – and where we found signs of even more unusual activities.

For example, the man was clearly interested in fire, and had several wooden stakes with pairs of tights wrapped around one end, which were steeping in a large vat of some sort of solvent in the basement. There were also several paintings depicting bodies burning on funeral pyres and people clutching similar burning stakes.

The police told us that the man had burn marks on the skin on the inner aspects of his legs and sides of his face. So it looked as though the stakes were used to re-enact some sort of fire-related fantasy – which might also explain the pile of mostly exotic women's clothing in a locked room upstairs, which he had clearly been wearing for some sexual activity.

Matters were temporarily confused by the discovery of several bowls of blood-soaked tissues that we found around the house – until we discovered that the man had had all his teeth taken out the previous day. And, in the end, there was nothing to suggest that he might be the Yorkshire Ripper.

I can remember a number of cases of auto-erotic asphyxiation, sometimes in bizarre circumstances, and often featuring a plastic bag over the head or a cord around the neck, or both, and sometimes with something in the mouth. In the UK, this is often ruled as 'death by misadventure' – i.e. resulting from someone taking a voluntary risk. One such case that sticks in my mind, which I didn't work on myself, but which I heard about at the time, involved the death of 45-year-old Conservative MP Stephen Milligan in 1994.

When Milligan's body was found in the kitchen of his house in London, he was wearing just a pair of tights and had a bin liner over his head and part of an orange in his mouth. After a post-mortem examination revealed that he had died of suffocation, and the coroner found no evidence to suggest that he had been murdered or committed suicide, the ruling at an inquest was 'death by misadventure'. But when it was subsequently revealed that Milligan had been involved in an investigation into illegal arms sales, some people began to wonder whether he had actually been murdered. For now, however, the original ruling stands.

It was a fetish for wearing rubber clothing that caused the death of 'the diver' in a very strange case that was investigated by forensic biologist Russell Stockdale.

At my desk in the office I set up at home for Forensic Access in 1986.

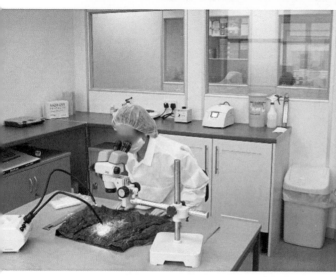

Inside biology search laboratories in the 1970s (top) and in 2021 (bottom).

Several layers of white paint and varnish on a damaged wooden surface at a crime scene (above), and a chip of matching painted and varnished wood found in the hood of a suspect's jacket (right).

A section through a chip of paint comprising eleven separate layers, each of a different colour, texture and chemical composition, and therefore capable of providing a very powerful evidential link.

Maltese-cross-shaped marks created by impact with the cartridge wadding in test fires (left), and examples of sawn-off shotguns (below), as in the case described in Chapter 13.

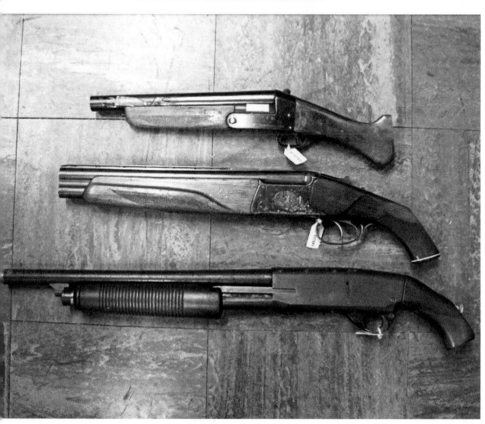

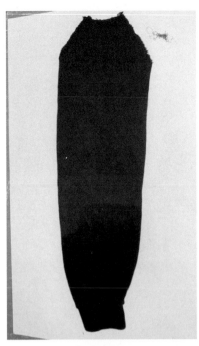

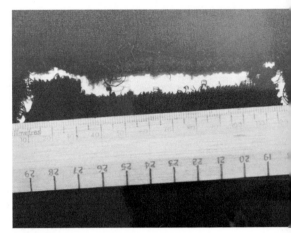

A mask made from the cut-off sleeve of a black jumper (left), and the physical fit between the sleeve and the hole in the jumper from which it came (below).

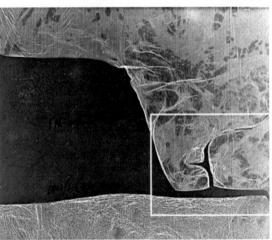

Links between the packaging of illicit drug samples and their suspected sources can involve physical fits in clingfilm (left) and stress marks (illuminated by polarised light – below).

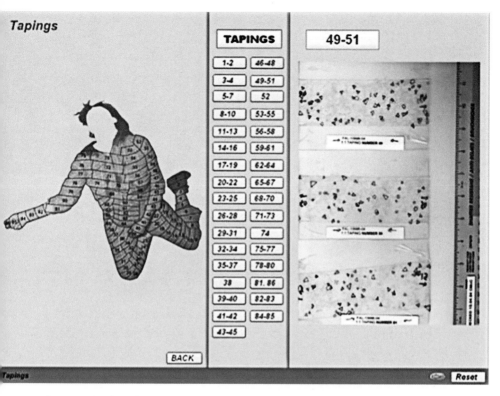

An example of one-to-one taping (or fibre mapping) in which every part of a victim's body is individually taped so that if any matching fibres are found on it, it is possible to say from precisely whereabouts on the body they were found.

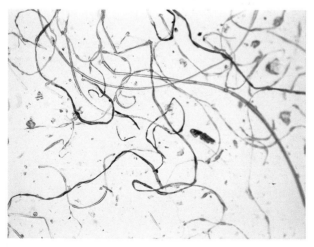

Debris including textile fibres and a host of other different types of particulate traces, such as DNA-containing body fluid and skin flakes, glass and soil particles, and paint and wood fragments, for example, which are commonly recovered on sticky-tape strips (tapings) taken from a wide variety of dry surfaces.

A mixture of wool, animal hair and nylon fibres in a reference sample from a knitted item of clothing as they appear under the microscope.

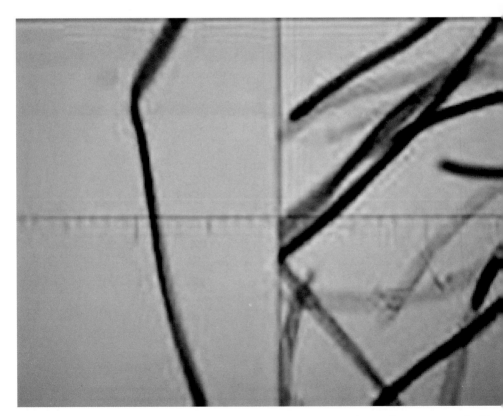

Comparing a textile fibre recovered from the clothing of a suspect (left) with a reference sample of fibres from the victim's clothing (right) under the microscope to see if they match.

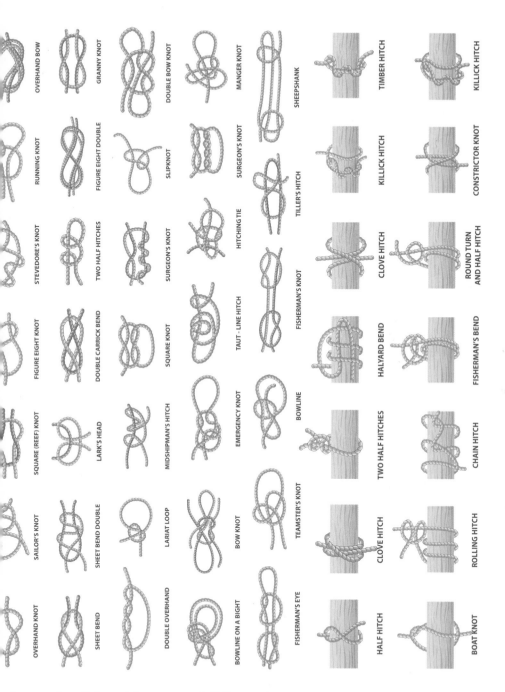

A sample of the wide range of different knots used in everyday life and therefore potentially significant in forensic casework.

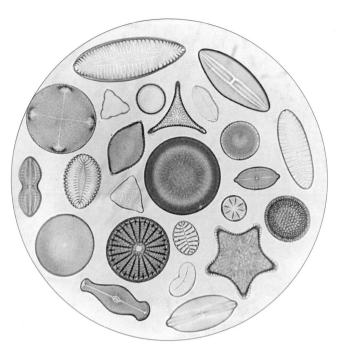

Examples of diatoms under the microscope illustrating a range of different forms.

Pollen grains of some common plant species.

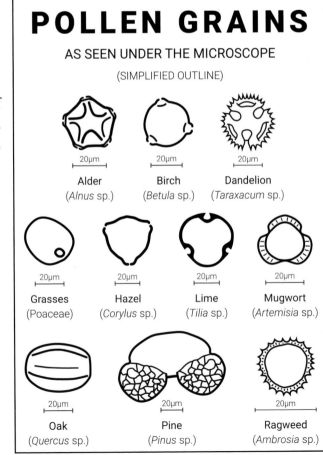

POLLEN GRAINS

AS SEEN UNDER THE MICROSCOPE

(SIMPLIFIED OUTLINE)

20μm

Alder
(*Alnus* sp.)

20μm

Birch
(*Betula* sp.)

20μm

Dandelion
(*Taraxacum* sp.)

20μm

Grasses
(Poaceae)

20μm

Hazel
(*Corylus* sp.)

20μm

Lime
(*Tilia* sp.)

20μm

Mugwort
(*Artemisia* sp.)

20μm

Oak
(*Quercus* sp.)

20μm

Pine
(*Pinus* sp.)

20μm

Ragweed
(*Ambrosia* sp.)

The police were already at the 'crime scene' when Russell arrived, and as they led him out of the back door of the house, he could see the wetsuit-clad body at the far end of the garden. The wetsuit itself appeared to be made out of various rubber items, including the inner tubes of bicycle tyres. The dead man's face was covered in a helmet-shaped mask with a pair of goggles attached. And a small spigot in the mouth area was linked to a narrow-bore tube that snaked the length of the garden and into the kitchen at the back of the house.

There was a small air pump on the floor in the kitchen, of the kind that was once used to oxygenate the water in fish tanks. On this occasion, however, it had obviously been supplying air to the man in the wetsuit before the tube had somehow become detached from the pump. With no resistance against which to operate, the pump must have finally burned itself out.

As was subsequently confirmed by some mathematical calculations, the narrowness of the tube meant that when the pump was no longer actively forcing oxygen down it, the man wasn't able to get enough air to breathe. He had probably been partially asphyxiated anyway – as is common in sexual fetishes. And combined with the cumbersome, multi-layered construction of the homemade wetsuit, it was likely that he didn't have the strength to pull off his helmet-mask in order to be able to breathe normally.

After the body had been taken to the mortuary, the man's clothing could be examined more carefully as it was removed. The first thing that became obvious was that it consisted of three layers of various items. Beneath the first rubber suit was another one, and under that was a layer of clothing made of black nylon. On his hands, there were three pairs of rubber gloves, secured at the wrists by rubber bands. His rubberised footwear was also secured with rubber bands, which were looped around the bottom of his rubber trousers. Also, in the urine-filled cavity between the two layers of his rubber boxer shorts was one end of a tube, the other end of which had been inserted into his penis.

There were signs elsewhere in the house that the dead man had been a competent engineer. For example, in the sitting room, which he had clearly been using as a workshop, there were working models of steam engines, lathes and various other bits of machinery. The sitting-room carpet was covered in metal filings and engine oil; and under one of the rubber cushions on the chairs there was a bowl of urine. In the bedroom, there were white rubber sheets on the bed, another bowl of urine on a shelf beside it, and a gas mask on the bedside table.

There was no mystery about the cause of death at the inquest into the case of 'the diver'. But sometimes it's a completely unconnected and innocent bystander who becomes the victim of someone's fetish, as occurred in a case that began with the disappearance in 1993 from the city of Potenza in southern Italy of sixteen-year-old Elisa Claps.

The chief suspect was a local man called Danilo Restivo, who was a friend of Elisa's and the last person to have been seen with her, at a church in Potenza. Restivo was known to have a fetish that involved surreptitiously cutting off locks of women's hair as they travelled on buses. But without a body, and with insufficient evidence to make an arrest, Elisa's disappearance remained a mystery.

One day almost a decade later, in November 2002, two children returned from school to their home in Bournemouth, on the south coast of England, to discover their mother's body in the bathroom. Heather Barnett had been bludgeoned to death with a hammer, her breasts had been cut off, and in each of her hands she held a lock of hair, only one of which was shown by forensic testing to be her own. The hair in her right hand was cut at both ends, and isotope analysis suggested that it had come from someone who had recently spent a short time in Florida and Southern Europe. It was considered possible that it had been placed in Heather's right hand deliberately by the offender, but no match was ever found for it.

One of the neighbours who rushed to help Heather's distraught children when they discovered their mother's body was an Italian man who had lived across the road for only a few months, and whose name was Danilo Restivo.

It turned out that Restivo had been to Heather's house during the preceding weeks to discuss with her some curtains he wanted her to make for him, and it was shortly after his visit, Heather's son reported, that they discovered their house keys had gone missing. When samples of blood from a green, bloodstained towel that had been found at the scene were tested by scientists at the FSS, the only DNA profiles they found matched Heather herself. So although Restivo was briefly a suspect, there was no evidence to implicate him in the killing.

The police did subsequently put Restivo under surveillance, and interviewed him in relation to numerous reports of women and young girls in the Bournemouth area having had locks of their hair surreptitiously cut off. But, again, there was no evidence to link him to the various cases.

During a re-investigation into the death of Heather Barnett in 2007, some skin flakes were found on tapings that had been taken from the green towel during the initial investigation. When these were tested, they provided a major DNA profile matching Heather's and a minor profile matching Restivo's. When presented with this evidence, Restivo claimed to have taken the towel to the house as a colour match for the curtains Heather was going to make for him. And he might have got away with all of it if Elisa Claps' body had not finally been found in March 2010 in the loft of the church in Italy where she had last been seen with him.

Within weeks of the discovery of Elisa's body, Danilo Restivo was arrested in Bournemouth and charged with the murder of Heather Barnett. Unusually, the evidence related to the Elisa Claps case was allowed to be heard as part of the prosecution's case against him, on the basis of 'similarity of offence' evidence. This meant that Italian forensic experts and other witnesses could testify during the Heather Barnett case in relation to the presence of DNA matching Restivo's that had been found on Elisa's clothing.

In June 2011, after being tried and found guilty of murdering Heather Barnett, Restivo was given a whole-life sentence, reduced to forty years on appeal. A few months later, at a trial that was conducted in his absence in Italy, he was also found guilty of murdering Elisa Claps, for which he received another prison sentence of thirty years.

Many fetishes don't affect other people and are simply activities in which some individuals like to indulge in the privacy of their own homes. At the other end of the scale, however, and when they involve other people, some fetishes can be deadly. This means that, particularly when related to someone's death, it is always important for investigators – supported by forensic scientists – to ascertain what happened, so that it is possible to distinguish between a tragic accident and a cold-blooded murder.

20

Poisoning and toxicology

Some cases of death by poisoning that come to the attention of forensic scientists are accidental, and some are deliberate, as the result of either murder or suicide. There are also quite a number of cases every year of people claiming that they are being deliberately poisoned, or that someone poisoned a recently deceased relative. In the latter circumstances, it is often a family member who is suspected, and although no toxicological evidence is found in the majority of cases, the claims are always taken seriously and investigated.

Because there is no physical force required to poison someone, and, in many cases, no risk of physical danger to the person responsible, poisoners can sometimes be long gone by the time there is any suspicion that someone has been poisoned. So the role of forensic scientists in poisoning cases usually revolves around chemical analysis.

One very unusual case of poisoning that toxicologist Denise Stanworth helped to solve involved the death in January 2009 of a man called Lakhvinder Cheema.

Lakhvinder and his fiancée, Gurjeet Choongh, were at his house in Feltham, London, and had just eaten the remains of a curry left over from the night before, when he began to feel unwell. A little while later, with Gurjeet experiencing similar symptoms of numbness and vomiting, Lakhvinder phoned for an ambulance and told the operator that they had been poisoned by his ex-girlfriend.

A month before that incident, Lakhvinder had been hospitalised for a week suffering from sickness, the cause of which doctors had been unable to establish. Unfortunately, on this second occasion, he died within an hour of being admitted to hospital. And with Gurjeet having been placed in a medically induced coma, the race began to search for and identify a possible poison that might have been added to the curry.

Medics who treated the couple said that Lakhvinder had a strong heart, but that it was beating to a rhythm they had never encountered before. In fact, they thought he might have ingested the drug digitalis. (Digitalis is produced from the leaves of the common foxglove, *Digitalis purpurea*, and other plants, and is prescribed in the form of the cardiac glycoside digoxin to strengthen the contractions of the heart and treat atrial fibrillation and heart failure.)

At the laboratory in Culham, Oxfordshire, Denise ran all the usual drug screens on a sample of the curry the couple had been eating when they were taken ill. Initially, all she detected were the spices and chemicals in the pepper, chilli and other ingredients, which could be ruled out as potential causes of poisoning.

One of the witnesses interviewed by the police was a lodger in Lakhvinder's home, who claimed that a woman who had visited the house earlier in the day had been seen to take a container out of the fridge and open its lid, and that she'd had a bag of powder in her handbag. When the woman was identified as Lakhvinder's ex-girlfriend, Lakhvir Singh, she became the police's prime suspect.

Before Gurjeet was placed in a coma, she had been able to give a detailed description of her symptoms. And as soon as Denise heard that one of them was numbness of the mouth, she started searching the curry for aconite, using what was then the relatively new technique of liquid chromatography-mass spectrometry (LC-MS). First, though, she had to develop a new analytical method that would specifically detect the chemical aconitine, which is found in plants of the *Aconitum* species (common name monkshood) and is highly toxic to the heart and nervous system.

Using the new method, Denise picked up signals that were similar to, but not exactly the same as, those that would be obtained from the alkaloids in aconite. But even something only very slightly different from your control or standard cannot be considered to be a match in forensic science. So, in the process of searching for more information, she visited Kew Gardens, where she discovered that there was a range of different aconites, as well as instrumentation to analyse them.

With the help of a colleague in her laboratory who was using various LC-MS methods to look for different alkaloids, it became possible to identify the alkaloids in the curry as coming from Indian aconite in particular. This result was subsequently confirmed when scientists at Kew Gardens reached the same conclusion.

Indian aconite, also known as pseudo-aconite, is extremely toxic and is found specifically in the Indian monkshood species *Aconitum ferox*, which grows in the Himalayas in India. Coincidentally – perhaps – while on a visit to the area not long before the incident that resulted in Lakhvinder's death, the suspect had bought an aconite-based herbal concoction to treat a skin condition. By analysing samples from the curry, the bodies of the deceased and the surviving victim, and the bag of powder found in the suspect's handbag, Denise was able to show that the same chemical profile was obtained from all of them.

In February 2010, Lakhvir Singh was found guilty of murder and sentenced to a minimum of twenty-three years in prison.

Forensic toxicology is a specialised type of forensic chemistry that involves examining samples of body fluids, tissues and organs for different kinds of toxic chemicals, drug substances (both of abuse and medicines) and their metabolites. (Metabolites are the compounds the drugs or medicines turn into once they are inside the body.) While some metabolites are short lived, others take longer to turn into something else or to be eliminated from the body, which can help a forensic toxicologist to work out *when* a particular drug was taken.

Toxicology is also concerned with establishing the quantity of drugs and/or alcohol in someone's body in cases of possible overdose, and to judge impairment at the time of an offence, including, of course, suspected drug- or drink-driving.

One of the many cases that toxicologist Dr Alex Allan has worked on followed the death of 'Moors murderer' Myra Hindley, who was sixty years old and serving a prison sentence when she died in hospital in East Anglia in 2002.

At their trial in 1966, Myra Hindley and Ian Brady were described by the judge as 'two sadistic killers of the utmost depravity'. Brady was given three life sentences, to run concurrently, for the murders of ten-year-old Lesley Ann Downey, twelve-year-old John Kilbride and seventeen-year-old Edward Evans. Myra Hindley received two life sentences, for the murders of Lesley Ann Downey and Edward Evans, with a concurrent seven-year sentence for having harboured Brady knowing that he had also killed John Kilbride. In fact, the couple were believed to have sexually abused, tortured and killed five children. But only three of the bodies were eventually discovered on Saddleworth Moor, near Manchester.

By 2002, Hindley, who had been a heavy smoker for many years, was suffering from chronic obstructive pulmonary disease (COPD) and other serious health issues and was being treated with high levels of morphine. After her death

– from natural causes, according to official reports – conspiracy theories began to circulate suggesting that she had been deliberately killed, possibly by the administration of an overdose of morphine.

The suspicions that arose were apparently partly fuelled by the fact that a proposed law would strip the Home Secretary of the power to set minimum sentences, which would become instead the prerogative of judges. With Hindley having spent almost thirty-six years in prison, there was concern among the many people affected by her crimes that her repeated appeals against her life sentences would eventually prove successful. It was at that point that we became involved.

As tolerance to morphine can vary among different people by a factor of five, it is difficult to work out how much of the drug would constitute an overdose for any specific person. So that was something Alex had to bear in mind when he looked at samples taken during the post-mortem examination from the body of 'Christine Charlton'. (In view of Hindley's crimes and the sensitive nature of the investigation, it was thought by the police to be a sensible precaution to use a fictitious name on her medical notes and on the samples that were sent to the laboratory after her death.)

One type of sample that Alex requested in this case was vitreous humour. By creating a barrier between the blood and the eye, this gelatinous substance, which fills the eyeball behind the lens, prevents proteins entering the eye that could potentially obscure vision. In various other parts of the body, such as the liver, the process by which drugs and other substances are broken down into metabolites is catalysed by hydrolytic enzymes that are not present in the vitreous humour. Therefore substances such as drugs remain in this part of the eye in their original, complete form. So, by comparing the level in the vitreous humour of a drug such as morphine with its level in the liver, it is possible to work out how recently the drug was ingested.

When Alex examined, analysed and compared the samples taken from the body of 'Christine Charlton', it was clear that she'd had a dose of morphine not long before she died. As that seemed to coincide with when the nurses turned her in her bed – which they did regularly and which would have been a very painful experience for her without the administration of morphine – there was no evidence to suggest that she had been given an overdose of the drug. Indeed, at the inquest that was held in Suffolk in January 2003, it was revealed that Hindley had been taking at least twenty different drugs at the time of her death.

So in this case, unlike in the last example, toxicological testing along with other contextual information about Hindley's state of health and nursing routine helped to allay any fears that she might have been murdered, as opposed to confirming that she had been.

There have been several high-profile cases of deliberate poisoning during recent decades. One of these involved a Bulgarian called Georgi Markov, who had defected to London, where he worked as a writer and radio broadcaster, and was openly critical of the political regime in his homeland. In 1978, as Markov was walking over Waterloo Bridge, he felt a sharp pain in his right thigh. When he turned around, he saw a man holding a rolled-up umbrella, who apologised and got into a taxi.

Later, when Markov examined his leg, he saw a red puncture mark surrounded by an area of inflammation that became progressively more inflamed. After developing a high fever in the night, he was admitted to hospital, where X-rays were taken of his leg, but revealed nothing. Two days later, despite being given high doses of antibiotics, Georgi Markov died.

After his death, a section of flesh from around the wound in his thigh was sent to the government's Chemical Defence Establishment at Porton Down in Wiltshire. The laboratory does some forensic work when it might involve more obscure poisons, such as those used in state-sponsored terrorism. And when the leg tissue was examined, a tiny metal pellet was discovered, into which two holes had been drilled. This raised the suspicion that the pellet had contained some type of lethal substance – probably a chemical toxin – and had been injected into Markov's thigh by a gas gun hidden in the umbrella wielded by the man on the bridge.

The most likely toxin seemed to be a substance called ricin, which is derived from the castor oil bean. A very potent haemorrhagic poison that causes blood to leak into the tissues, ricin is 500 times more powerful than cyanide. But because it is broken down so quickly in the body, there is no reliable test to identify it. So an amount of ricin similar to the amount that could have been held in the metal pellet was injected into a pig, which suffered exactly the same sort of symptoms as Markov had done.

At an inquest in January 1979, the cause of Georgi Markov's death was given as toxaemia resulting from the implantation of a metal pellet containing ricin, which, the coroner stated, it was quite impossible for Mr Markov to have done himself. Who *was* responsible for implanting the fatal pellet has never been established.

Another case of deliberate poisoning involved the killing of former spy and officer of the Russian Federal Security Service (FSB) Alexander Litvinenko. After being arrested, tried and acquitted in Russia for criticising the FSB, Litvinenko fled to the UK with his family in the year 2000 and was granted asylum. In November 2006, he was admitted to hospital, where he died three weeks later from what turned out to be polonium-210 poisoning.

Polonium-210 – which it was thought had been administered to Litvinenko in a cup of tea – was discovered by Marie Curie in 1898. It is an extremely nasty radioactive poison that damages cellular material and is very dangerous if inhaled or ingested, but may be difficult to detect. The laboratory used for part of this work was LGC, which had its own forensics division at the time. It was not chosen because of that, however, but because one of its other specialities was in the analysis of water samples. And it was water in some of the drains under London that enabled the scientists to determine *where* – and therefore more about *how* – the poison had been delivered.

A public inquiry that was eventually held in the UK in 2015 concluded that Litvinenko had been killed by two Russian suspects who were 'probably' acting on behalf of the FSB. In September 2021, the European Court of Human Rights found Russia responsible for the assassination.

In another case, it was the potent organophosphorus nerve agent Novichok that caused the hospitalisation of Russian double agent Sergei Skripal and his daughter Yulia in March 2018. It turned out that the poison had been smeared on the front-door handle of their home in Salisbury, Wiltshire. And although the Skripals recovered, local resident Dawn Sturgess died later that year after apparently spraying herself from a Novichok-contaminated perfume bottle that had been found by her partner. Following an investigation, two Russian agents – and, more recently, a third – were identified as suspects, and are still wanted for questioning.

It was also Novichok that was thought to have been put in the boxer shorts of Russian opposition leader and lawyer Alexei Navalny by FSB agents while he was staying in a hotel in the Siberian town of Tomsk in August 2020. After boarding a flight to Moscow wearing the poisoned underpants, Navalny became ill, and the plane made an emergency landing in Omsk. What probably saved his life was the fact that he was quickly transferred to hospital, and subsequently flown on to Berlin for treatment. After returning to Russia in January

2021, he was sentenced to two and half years in a labour camp on an earlier charge of embezzlement.

A few years earlier, in February 2017, it was another banned organophosphorus nerve agent called VX that caused the death of North Korean leader Kim Jong-un's half-brother, Kim Jong-nam. The poison was thought to have been splashed on to the victim while he was in Kuala Lumpur International Airport in Malaysia. Two female suspects who were charged with the offence – one Indonesian and the other Vietnamese – claimed to have thought they were taking part in a TV show. Murder charges against both women were subsequently dropped, and one of them served just a short prison sentence after being found guilty of a lesser charge.

As well as being used to quell voices of dissent, organophosphorus nerve agents are sometimes used in terrorist attacks, such as those involving the nerve gas sarin that occurred on the subway in Tokyo on 20 March 1995. Carried out by a terrorist and doomsday cult organisation, the five co-ordinated attacks that took place during the rush hour that day killed thirteen people and injured thousands more.

It turned out that the same organisation had been responsible for another sarin attack the previous year in the Japanese city of Matsumoto. This had resulted in the deaths of eight people and injuries to 500.

Many members of the cult were later arrested, thirteen of whom, including its leader, were found guilty and executed, while many more received prison sentences of varying lengths.

The range of poisons used to commit murder and suicide is wide. When coal gas was still in domestic use in the UK prior to the 1970s, the fact that it contained carbon monoxide made it a favoured method of poisoning for both suicides and murders. The carbon monoxide in car exhaust fumes was another source of poisoning before the introduction of catalytic converters in the mid-1970s, and their subsequent mandatory use in cars manufactured since 1993.

Plant poisons tend to be favoured by people from countries with traditional medicine systems, such as China and India. Those with medical knowledge (for example, chemists) and agricultural workers will probably pick the tools of their trade, and others will use whatever medicines or household products come easily to hand. All of which makes it important for toxicologists and other forensic investigators examining this type of case to know as much about the circumstances of the poisoning and the perpetrator as possible.

Serial killer and doctor Harold Shipman favoured opiates, which are difficult to identify as the cause of death in elderly patients rendered vulnerable by illnesses and other medicines. Cyanide was used in the murders and suicides of more than 900 men, women and children in the Jonestown cult settlement in Guyana on 18 November 1978. The poisoning of children by their parents or carers often involves prescribed medicines, or drugs of abuse such as heroin or methadone. While Beverley Allitt chose insulin to kill and injure children in the hospital in Lincolnshire where she was working as a nurse.

Allitt was apparently suffering from the mental health disorder Munchausen syndrome by proxy when she was found guilty in 1993 of four counts of murder, eleven counts of attempted murder, and eleven counts of causing grievous bodily harm to children on the hospital ward where she worked. And it was when one mother's condition escalated from Munchausen syndrome to Munchausen syndrome by proxy that she caused the tragic death of her own young son.

When nine-year-old David Stocker was admitted to hospital in Romford, Essex, in March 2001 suffering from stomach pains, doctors were baffled by his symptoms. As the little boy's condition deteriorated over the next few months, he was treated in Romford and at Great Ormond Street Children's Hospital in London for vomiting, lethargy and significant loss of weight that eventually confined him to a wheelchair.

Every time David was admitted to hospital, his mother, Petrina, stayed with him, and she was at his bedside in Great Ormond Street when he was diagnosed with PANDAS syndrome. An autoimmune neuropsychiatric infection that is triggered in a small number of children by common strepto-coccal infections such as 'strep throat', PANDAS syndrome is usually quickly controlled by the type of anti-viral medication that was given to David Stocker via intravenous infusion at the hospital. But despite this treatment, David wasn't showing any signs of getting better.

Eventually, nursing staff noticed that David's condition seemed to deteriorate whenever his mother was around. Shortly after they had begun to suspect that she was interfer-ing with his treatment, cloudy fluid was discovered in the fluid line delivering the anti-viral drug, and his urine samples were found to contain blood.

When Petrina Stocker heard that there was a plan to move her son's bed nearer to the nurses' station, she threatened to remove him from the hospital. Not long afterwards, in August 2001, David died.

When samples from the body were analysed by eminent chemical pathologist Dr Robert Forrest, they showed that David had been suffering from ketosis and had been poisoned by salt. (Ketosis is a state characterised by raised levels in the blood and urine of molecules called ketones, which are produced by the liver in response to fasting or starvation.)

Dr Alex Allan was then asked to carry out further investiga-tions on a large number of samples collected from Petrina Stocker's kitchen, as well as on body samples from her son. The main purpose of his investigations was to ascertain whether there was anything else that could have accounted for the cloudiness of the fluid drip line and for the blood in David's urine.

At first, Alex's discovery of acetone (a type of ketone) in many of the samples seemed unremarkable. But as well as being produced by the liver, acetone is a type of solvent that is present in many cleaning materials used in homes and laboratories – and it was on a list that Alex had been given of the chemicals Petrina Stocker had access to during her work at a school. The fact that acetone precipitates protein in solution meant that, in principle, it could have been what caused the cloudiness in the fluid drip line.

In the end, it turned out that Petrina Stocker had done numerous things over a five-month period that were designed to produce symptoms in her son in order to gain attention – by proxy – for herself. But it was the addition of thirteen teaspoons of salt to his hospital drip that had caused his brain to swell and resulted in his death.

Following a three-month trial at the Old Bailey in London, which ended in February 2005 and involved 150 witnesses for the prosecution – including Alex – Petrina Stocker was found guilty of manslaughter and sentenced to five years in prison. After the verdict was announced, it was revealed that she had made false claims about her own health some twenty years earlier. These included adding sugar to a urine sample to support her false assertion that she had diabetes, and scarring her face and arms with acid after claiming to have leukaemia.

Not all cases of poisoning are deliberate, of course, and poisons can also feature in industrial accidents and during the normal course of certain jobs. For example, the highly toxic gas arsine, which is produced by the reaction of arsenic to acid, is a by-product of various metal industries. If inhaled, it causes the rupture of red blood cells, resulting in anaemia and kidney failure; a week later, arsenic will begin to show up in the hair.

Another form of poisoning can result from fumes from a hydraulic leak escaping into the closed cockpit of an aeroplane. This can occur with petrol engines, which, unlike jet engines, are at the front of the plane and provide heat for the inside. And it was apparently just such a leak that caused the light aircraft carrying the Argentinian football player Emiliano Sala to crash into the English Channel on 21 January 2019.

Although the body of the pilot, David Ibbotson, has not been found, Sala's body was retrieved from the wreckage that was discovered on the seabed two weeks after the small Piper Malibu aircraft disappeared. When tested, Sala's body was found to have a carbon-monoxide level of 48–50 per cent. As anything above 10–20 per cent has an effect on judgement and behaviour, it seems likely that carbon-monoxide poisoning was also a factor in any errors that might have been made by the pilot.

Sometimes, the police use sniffer dogs that have been trained to smell certain drugs and poisons. But it isn't a skill that is restricted only to dogs. Some humans can do it too, which was particularly useful for providing a heads-up on what to look for – in samples of stomach contents and contaminated drinks or foodstuffs, for example – in the days before drug-analysis instruments were as sensitive as they are today.

People's perception of smell and sensitivity to smells differ significantly, and what is particularly relevant for a forensic scientist is the fact that the ability to detect the odour of cyanide is genetically determined. In one spot check, cyanide could be smelled by approximately 50 per cent of people in a laboratory, but not by the other 50 per cent.

Knowing that you're a 'non-smeller' could be potentially useful in keeping you out of harm's way, because one of the various forms in which cyanide exists is as hydrogen cyanide, which turns from a liquid to a highly poisonous gas above room temperature. Cyanide in the form of its sodium or potassium salts has been used in criminal poisoning cases, threats and suicides, and hydrogen cyanide is produced when the salts interact with gastric acid in the stomach. Because it is so toxic by inhalation, it is necessary to check that staff are able to detect it before sniffing stomach contents during forensic investigations into suspicious deaths.

Other examples of substances that may be readily recognised by smell in stomach contents include alcohol, white spirit, turpentine, various pesticides such as certain weedkillers, and the sedative drug chlormethiazole, which is used to treat the symptoms of acute alcohol withdrawal but is highly toxic in overdose. Sniffing suspected contaminated drinks and foodstuffs also sometimes gives us a lead on malicious contamination, e.g. urine in cola.

It isn't just in cases of suspected poisoning that being a 'smeller' can prove useful, however. In a project that Alex Allan worked on abroad during a period of civil unrest, he could smell acetic acid on some samples connected to bombs he was examining. His heightened sense of smell proved extremely useful on that occasion, because it indicated the type of explosive they were dealing with. But it failed to impress one of the scientists working in the laboratory, who looked at him with an expression of barely concealed disapproval when he realised what he was doing, and then remarked stiffly, 'But only dogs sniff!'

As the sixteenth-century German-Swiss physician known as Paracelsus famously remarked: 'All substances are poisonous, the only thing that distinguishes them is the dose.' This is reflected in the enormously wide range of substances – from the rarest of poisons to the most commonplace of domestic chemicals or even foodstuffs – that toxicologists can find themselves analysing when faced with an unexplained or suspicious death.

But it isn't just the substance itself that has to be identified. As with all other areas of forensic endeavour, it is also the how, when, where and by whom the substance could have been administered that are key to distinguishing between accidental and deliberate poisoning, and therefore tragic accident, murder and suicide.

21

Quality control and contamination

However rigorous the processes and procedures, however many checks and balances have been put in place, and however conscientious the practitioner in any walk of life, mistakes do sometimes occur. In some situations, these simply cause irritation and inconvenience. But a mistake made by a forensic scientist has the potential to result in the wrongful conviction and loss of freedom of an innocent person, or the acquittal of a killer who might go on to kill again.

The majority of the mistakes made by forensic scientists that have come to light have been accidental – the result of inappropriate handling of exhibits, by either scientists or police officers, or inadvertent misinterpretation of results through lack of knowledge about context, for example. In one instance, however, it was the deliberate manipulation of the results of forensic testing by some scientists at a company called Randox that led to the wrongful convictions of numerous motorists on drug-driving offences. The reasons why the scientists involved acted as they did have been the subject of much speculation, but may become clearer following publication of the report of an investigation by the Forensic Science Regulator.

One example of a genuine error involved the inadvertent re-use of disposable plastic sample trays in the DNA-profiling process, which came to light when a man was charged with rape in a city to which he insisted he had never been. A sample from the victim produced a profile that matched the suspect's reference sample on the National DNA Database. But it turned out that the suspect's sample had been processed earlier in the same laboratory in connection with another matter entirely, and that the sample well in the re-used tray was the one that had held his previous sample. In fact, the same sort of error had occurred subsequently in the same laboratory in another batch of trays. On that occasion, it had been spotted and procedures had been rectified, but there had been insufficient back-tracking to see if it had ever happened before.

In another instance, the wrong sample was submitted to the laboratory by the police when they were investigating two burglaries. This resulted in the victim from the first burglary being arrested for the second. On this occasion, it was discovered that the critical samples had been given the same exhibit reference number, although other details about their provenance were obviously different. When someone from the laboratory rang up to query this, the police said that there had been only one sample taken in the second case and told the lab to carry on, which they did – although that wasn't quite the point. Again, recommendations for adjustments to procedures were made, both in terms of submissions of items to the laboratory concerned, and communications between the lab and the police.

A third case involved a handling error in a laboratory when, again, one sample was DNA-profiled twice, and a second sample wasn't profiled at all. This resulted in someone being charged with two burglaries instead of one. Once again, recommendations for improvements were made to avoid the same thing happening in the future. But it was another example of a case highlighting the dangers of accepting things, even quality-controlled scientific results, at face value.

Because such errors can – and do – occur, it is essential for any provider of forensic services to have a rigorous system of quality management in place. Robust quality systems are absolutely key to every aspect of forensic science, so that the scientists themselves know they are doing things correctly, and so that other people can also have confidence in their results.

There are two main aspects of quality. Quality control ensures that all activities carried out in forensic laboratories meet recognised standards for the accurate, robust and impartial support of criminal justice. Quality assurance is about demonstrating this through monitoring, regular assessment and record keeping, and providing evidence of continual improvement.

With cost an increasingly limiting factor, quality systems also ensure that the work is done as effectively and efficiently as possible. The fact that at least independent forensic laboratories in the UK need to have accreditation to internationally recognised standards set by the International Organization for Standardization (ISO) also allows for international co-operation for cross-border crime and data sharing.

While accreditation of police in-house forensic units has been gradually catching up with the independent suppliers, they are not there yet. So we still cannot assume that all forensic science presented to our courts has been produced in a properly quality-assured and controlled environment. On top of this, there are the much more subtle risks of cognitive bias. In simple terms, cognitive bias occurs when someone's judgements and conclusions are influenced by their prior knowledge. This is a particular concern in view of the fact that the police are increasingly doing their own forensic work – in effect, setting and marking their own homework – especially when their budgets for forensics are under such constant pressure. And, as we've seen, even with quality systems in place, it is still perfectly possible for genuine mistakes to be made, and these are usually uncovered by checks performed on behalf of the defence. But the point about quality management systems is that you learn from your mistakes.

Another very important risk that rigorous quality control helps to minimise is that of contamination. Forensic evidence often focuses on the transfer of trace materials you can't necessarily see, such as blood and DNA on to clothing, door handles and vehicle interiors, for example, and of textile fibres, hairs (both human and animal), flakes of paint and tiny fragments of glass. Contamination with something before or after an incident can lead to the mistaken conclusion that there is an evidential link between certain items and/or specific people. So before it is safe to conclude that this type of transfer is necessarily evidence of contact during the commission of a crime, it is important to consider whether it could alternatively have been the result of accidental contamination subsequently or, indeed, of legitimate contact some time previously.

One such experience occurred some years ago while working on a re-investigation, when we found some unusual purple acrylic fibres that appeared to provide a link between the victim and a suspect. When the original laboratory was informed of our discovery, something struck a chord with them. And after a bit of local investigation, they told us they had established that the fibres had actually come from a purple jumper worn by a member of their staff, which apparently shed its constituents very freely. Although the staff member had left the laboratory some two years previously, some of the fibres were still to be found in the locker she had used – and some had also clearly spread all over their laboratory.

In some situations, the potential for legitimate contact should become apparent during the police enquiries. But the need to avoid accidental contamination must be a major consideration from the outset for everyone involved in the investigation. This involves choosing access routes into and out of a crime scene that avoid any potentially significant areas such as entry and exit routes used by the perpetrator, and putting up tapes to protect them. A log is also kept of everyone entering and leaving the crime scene. So if there is any doubt about who might have left a set of footwear marks, for example, it is relatively easy to eliminate everyone with legitimate access to the scene. Or if a particular officer both went to a crime scene *and* helped to apprehend a suspect shortly afterwards, this can be authoritatively confirmed.

Forensic scientists have to be very careful not to leave behind anything of themselves at crime scenes – such as the traces mentioned above – that could be picked up and mistaken for evidence. So, as well as wearing all-in-one 'bunny suits', masks, gloves and overshoes at crime scenes, they also have to guard against the risk of contamination in the laboratory. Here, white coats are routinely worn, and these are increasingly likely to be disposable, and teamed with similarly disposable hair nets, masks and gloves, as well as overshoes or washable clogs. To avoid leaving fingerprints, forensic scientists wear two pairs of gloves – a cotton inner pair with a latex or vinyl pair on top. In some situations – such as when DNA might be involved, the tiniest traces of which can produce a result – they may also wear surgeon-style scrubs under their lab coats, instead of their own clothes.

Other precautions in the laboratory include complete separation of examinations of the victim's and suspect's clothing, and of other items and samples relating to them; strict adherence to lab protocols that support this; and seemingly endless laboratory cleaning routines. Continual improvements to such precautions have been made over the years, informed by research and experience.

One case of contamination that apparently caused some difficulties for the police occurred in a laboratory involved in the forensic investigation into the death of MI6 agent Gareth Williams in 2010.

After Williams' naked body was found in a locked holdall in his flat in London, the lab reported the presence of an unknown DNA profile. This information sent the Metropolitan Police off on a wild goose chase, before it was realised that the profile in question was actually from one of the lab's own scientists. Contamination of this sort is an occupational hazard, especially with the increasing sensitivity of DNA tests. But it is normally dealt with before any information is sent to the police by comparing any DNA profiles obtained with a database containing those of all laboratory staff.

In 2012, the coroner's verdict was that Williams had been unlawfully killed by persons unknown. But in 2013, the Metropolitan Police said that he had probably died by accident after getting in to the bag on his own. However, some people believe that stories of Williams' interest in bondage and auto-erotic activities were exaggerated and that his death was related to his apparent involvement in an investigation of international money-laundering routes.

In cold-case re-investigations, the opportunity for accidental contamination tends to be magnified, for example by the number of times an item has been taken in and out of its bag and re-examined, possibly over quite an extended period of time and in different locations by different people. This was particularly relevant in times past, when lab protocols were less stringent than they need to be today with our modern technology that can analyse traces you can't even see with the naked eye.

Also, of course, although very rare, there is the possibility of deliberate contamination. Normally, this should be relatively straightforward to detect, as it will almost certainly be at odds with the scientist's expectations. And as scientists are constantly alert to this possibility, they will sometimes check with a senior officer in the force who is outside the immediate investigation if they think something could conceivably be awry.

22

Returning to the scene of a crime

Why *do* some criminals return to the scene of their crime? In the case of an arsonist, it might be for the satisfaction of seeing the 'fruits of their labours', as firefighters battle to extinguish the flames and save the terrified residents of burning homes. Bomb makers might want to see for themselves the damage that has been caused by the explosion, so that they can identify ways of 'improving' a bomb's design for the next time. Some criminals might enjoy the feeling of power it gives them to see how their actions have affected the lives of others. Or maybe it's a way of keeping tabs on what the police officers and forensic scientists are doing as they try to work out what happened and how to find the person(s) responsible.

There are reasons, too, why burglars might return to the scene of a crime, often a few weeks later, when the burgled person has had enough time to replace the items that were burgled on the first attempt. Or maybe there were items the burglar noticed but couldn't take with them the first time, which will also be easier to steal now that they know the layout of the property and the security measures that are in place.

Sometimes though, returning to the scene of their crime is what seals a criminal's fate.

In October 1986, the bodies of Karen Hadaway and Nicola Fellows were discovered in woodland near Brighton. The little girls were just nine years old, and had been sexually assaulted and strangled. A year later, a twenty-year-old local man called Russell Bishop was tried for their murders, but acquitted when the evidence against him proved to be ambiguous.

When Bishop was subsequently identified by the seven-year-old victim of another attack, a young forensic biologist working for the FSS at the time, Roy Green, found semen and other body fluids that linked Bishop and his surviving victim to a pair of discarded jogging bottoms. In 1990, Bishop was convicted of offences related to this attack, which involved attempted murder, kidnapping and indecent assault, and was sentenced to a minimum of fourteen years in prison.

Apparently, it was Bishop's habit to throw away any potentially incriminating clothing he had been wearing when he committed his offences. And some thirty years later, it was Roy again – working this time as an established part of the cold-case team I set up at LGC Forensics (now Eurofins) – who discovered DNA and fibre evidence linking Bishop to a sweatshirt that was found at the scene of the 1986 murders.

Bishop's desire to return to the scene of the crime – for whatever reason – had resulted in him taking part in the original search for Nicola and Karen. So it was a theoretically plausible defence that his DNA and fibres from his sweatshirt had been transferred to their bodies then, and specifically when he claimed he touched them in order to feel for a pulse after they were found. But it was a claim that was disputed by two witnesses, who said that he could not have got that close to the bodies. And in October 2018, Russell Bishop was found guilty of the murders of the two little girls who had become known as 'the babes in the wood' and jailed for life.

Another reason for criminals returning to the scene of their crimes is the realisation that they may have left behind them some potentially incriminating evidence. That was a thought that apparently struck the Yorkshire Ripper as he was driving from Manchester to his home in Bradford on the evening of 1 October 1977.

As noted in the Byford Report that followed a subsequent inquiry into police handling of the Yorkshire Ripper murder investigation, Peter Sutcliffe picked up Jean Jordan in the red-light district of Manchester's Moss Side at around 9 p.m. that night. After giving her the agreed advance payment of £5, he followed her directions and drove with her to a patch of wasteland adjacent to some allotments in the suburb of Chorlton. While Jean got out of the car and started walking into the darkness, Sutcliffe took a hammer out of the boot, walked up behind her and struck her with it eleven times on the head.

As he was crouching over the body, someone in a car that was parked nearby turned on the headlights and started the engine. So Sutcliffe dragged his victim towards some bushes, then got back into his own car and set off on the fifty-mile (80-km) drive home.

It was during that drive that he remembered the crisp, newly minted £5 note he had given Jean Jordan earlier that night, and that he himself had received in his pay packet a couple of days earlier. Realising that he would increase his chance of being noticed if he returned immediately to the scene of his crime, Sutcliffe decided to wait and see what happened. But, apparently, he had hidden the body well, and when it hadn't been discovered ten days later, he drove back to the patch of wasteland to retrieve the money.

According to what he told police later, after locating Jean's body where he had left it, Sutcliffe searched for her handbag, which was nowhere to be found. Then, partly to vent his rage, and partly in an attempt to avoid any link to the *modus operandi* of the Yorkshire Ripper, he stripped off her clothes and searched them before stabbing and slashing her corpse repeatedly with a knife.

That same morning, the body was finally discovered. A few days later, Jean's handbag was also found, lying open after possibly having already been searched by someone else before Sutcliffe tried to find it. And concealed in a small, outer, side pocket of the handbag was a very wet £5 note.

The note was quickly identified from its serial number as one of a batch sent from the Bank of England to branches of the Midland Bank in Shipley and Bingley, near Bradford. Four days before Jean Jordan was murdered, it had been issued by the sub-branch in Shipley as part of a batch that was split up and given to various local factories and businesses to be paid out as wages to their workers on 29 and 30 September.

It seemed extremely unlikely that the £5 note had travelled from Shipley to Manchester (where it was found) through the usual commercial routes in only two days, at most. So if the police could trace the man who had received it in his pay packet, they would probably have Jean Jordan's killer – and quite possibly the killer of the ten or eleven other women who, by that time, were thought to have been brutally injured or murdered by the Yorkshire Ripper.

Unfortunately, to cut a regrettably protracted story short, the police waited too long to reveal to the public why they had been interviewing the 8,000 men who worked at the thirty factories and businesses that had received notes from the batch in question. So the opportunity to identify the killer was lost.

Two years later, when the number of potentially involved businesses had been whittled down to three and the number of workers to 360, another attempt was made to identify the original owner of the £5 note. But, once again, Peter Sutcliffe somehow managed to slip through the investigative net.

As the Byford Report later stated, if the police had made public their search for the original recipient of the £5 note as soon as they knew the serial number they were looking for, someone might have come forward with information. Then Sutcliffe might have been identified two or three years before he was eventually arrested and charged in January 1981. At his trial later that year, Peter Sutcliffe was found guilty of murdering thirteen women and attempting to kill seven more, and was serving a whole-life order when he died in prison in 2020.

Although Sutcliffe's intention was thwarted, the instinct to return to the scene of the crime made sense on that particular occasion – from the criminal's point of view. From the scientist's point of view, however, doing so simply provides further opportunity for criminals to leave behind, or pick up, additional incriminating traces, especially now that we have such sensitive and discriminating techniques at our disposal.

23

Serial offenders

It often isn't until there have been a few deaths that the police begin to realise they are dealing with a serial killer. This is because each case will inevitably be slightly different and, at the start, it is difficult to know what is different because someone else is responsible, and what is simply within the range of variation in one person's activities.

In fact, there is some discrepancy about what actually constitutes serial killing. The definition used by the UK Centre for Crime and Justice Studies, and closely echoed by the FBI in the US, is: 'The rarest form of homicide, occurring when an individual has killed three or more people who were previously unknown to him or her, with a "cooling off" period between each murder.' According to the US National Institute of Justice, however, in order to qualify as 'serial', the number of killings must be 'two or more', and they must be carried out with a psychological motive and sadistic sexual overtones.

Although the majority of serial killings may be sexually motivated, that isn't true of all of them. For example, there was no apparent sexual motive to the crimes committed by British GP Harold Shipman, who killed his victims by injecting them with lethal doses of painkillers. In 2004, Shipman hanged himself while serving a life sentence for the murder of fifteen of his patients, and may actually have been responsible for the deaths of more than 200 people.

Another fact about serial killers that may be contrary to common conception is that they are not always men. One of the first examples of a female serial killer that springs to mind is 'Moors murderer' Myra Hindley, who died in prison in 2002 while serving a life sentence for the murders of two little girls between 1963 and 1965.

I have been involved in one way or another with several investigations into serial killings since I started working for the FSS almost forty-seven years ago. The first dead body I ever saw was a victim of serial killer Peter Sutcliffe, who became known as 'the Yorkshire Ripper'. I was twenty-seven years old. It was 1978, and I was working at the FSS laboratory in Wetherby, West Yorkshire, when I attended the crime scene at a woodyard in Huddersfield where eighteen-year-old Helen Rytka had been murdered.

Fourteen months later, I attended another Yorkshire Ripper crime scene, this time in Halifax, where Sutcliffe had killed nineteen-year-old Josephine Whitaker as she was walking home through a park one night.

When it became apparent that we were dealing with a serial killer, we went back through our old cases to see if we could identify when he first started. What we decided was that his first victim was likely to have been Olive Smelt, who was seriously injured but survived when he attacked her in August 1975 with a sock containing heavy stones – which was different from the hammer he used in subsequent assaults. When the police went through the same process, however, they showed that the Yorkshire Ripper had actually attacked his first victim a few years earlier, in 1969. On that occasion, he had also used a sock with a stone in it. But the weapons used for his assault on his second victim, the month before he attacked Olive Smelt, were a hammer and a knife.

Despite the exceptional lengths the FSS went to in an attempt to find anything that might help to identify the killer, our tools at the time were fairly basic, and it was two police officers who eventually helped to solve the case (see Chapter 15).

Not all serial offenders are killers, of course, and it was a series of rapes committed in the Barnsley area of Yorkshire that also occupied the attention of West Yorkshire Police in the 1970s.

I was one of a number of scientists who became involved in the forensic investigation into the rapes committed by the man who had become known as 'the Barnsley Beast'. It was 1975, and I had been working for the FSS for just over a year when I was given various items to examine in relation to the first of the two rapes in the series that I was asked to look at. These included items of clothing from the victim and some soil and bark samples from the scene.

I found seminal staining on three items of clothing, and also recovered surface debris from all of the items, in case there might be an opportunity in the future to compare any textile fibres in it with the constituents of the clothing from any suspect that might emerge from police enquiries.

In addition, I examined a piece of bark from a tree at the scene into which I understood the victim had said her attacker had stuck the knife with which he had been threatening her. During my examination I noticed that the bark contained a split measuring approximately three inches (8 cm) in length down its long axis. When I pressed the two sides of this split firmly together, I saw that it left a thin slot in its centre approximately three-quarters of an inch (2 cm) in length, and I suggested that such a slot could have been produced by the insertion of a knife blade into the bark. In other words, this provided some corroboration for the victim's account of events.

The second case – involving another victim – occurred in September 1976. The items submitted this time included the victim's clothing, samples of vegetation, saliva and pubic hair, as well as vulval and vaginal swabs. I found semen on the intimate swabs, which indicated that she had had recent sexual intercourse, and also seminal stains on the insides of every item of her clothing and even on the outside of one of her boots. I took samples of the staining on two of these items and subjected them to ABO secretor grouping tests, which were pretty much all we had for semen in 1976. But in neither case did I detect any blood-group substance – indicating that the semen had come from a 'non-secretor' individual. (Basically, everyone has an ABO group, but whereas everyone secretes their ABO-group substance(s) into their blood, not everyone – the 'non-secretors' – does so into other body fluids such as semen.)

Other evidence of the attack the second victim had suffered consisted of some damage to her clothing, small amounts of vegetation and soil staining, and small bloodstains that could have come from her. I also collected surface debris from the clothing, as I had done for the previous case.

Later on in 1976, when Reginald Chapman became a suspect, the police sent a sample of his saliva into the lab for testing and comparison, and this showed that he was a 'non-secretor'. A number of items of his clothing that were also submitted allowed me to compare their constituent fibres with the textile fibres in the surface debris I had earlier recovered from the two victims' clothes. In each case, this produced some very useful evidence of a link. In particular, from the debris from the second victim's clothing, I recovered no fewer than 178 brown acrylic fibres that matched the constituent fibres of one of Chapman's jumpers. I also discovered three dark-green acrylic fibres that matched numerous fibres of the same type found on the surface of his clothing. In relation to the first victim, the fibre evidence consisted of thirty-one red viscose fibres and four red polyester fibres which could all have come from a pair of Chapman's trousers.

Although my witness statements were used when the case went to court, I didn't give evidence in person, as I had been ill and so couldn't attend until late in the proceedings, by which time my oral evidence wasn't required. Although the defendant, Reginald George Chapman, had already confessed his guilt, he must have subsequently changed his mind, as the trial went ahead and he was convicted of multiple charges of rape and given a life sentence eight times over.

A few months later, Ron Outerridge – who was my boss at the FSS at the time – received a letter from Chapman in which he asked some very technical questions about the forensic evidence connected with the one or two cases with which Ron had been involved. Ron answered the letter with some carefully worded explanations. But by the time I received a similar letter in 1982, the FSS had decided it was pointless entering into correspondence with Chapman. So I answered by suggesting that he should appeal his conviction in the usual way.

In 1985, Chapman's new probation officer rang the FSS lab at Wetherby and asked to speak to another scientist who worked on some of the other cases. When he was told that that particular scientist was no longer working there, the probation officer asked for his contact details, and was advised to follow the suggestion in my previous letter and to petition the Home Office for an appeal if he had concerns about his conviction.

The position was very different by the time my colleagues and I were invited to become part of the cold-case investigation of what became known as the Pembrokeshire Coastal Path Murders. As well as DNA, we had much more sophisticated forms of other types of analysis too.

We were asked initially to carry out a forensic re-investigation of the deaths of husband and wife Peter and Gwenda Dixon, who had been shot at close range while walking on the Pembrokeshire Coastal Path in Wales in 1989. Helping to solve that crime led to confirmation that the same person had also been responsible for the deaths some four years earlier of brother and sister Richard and Helen Thomas in their remote farmhouse in the same general area, as well as for the rape and sexual assault at gunpoint of two young girls near Milford Haven in 1996. And in 2011, serial killer John Cooper was found guilty on all counts and sentenced to life in prison.

Cooper was a prolific burglar, and had only just been released from prison for armed robbery and burglary-related crimes when he was re-arrested for the Dixons' murders. Part of his *modus operandi* as a burglar was to discard stolen goods he didn't want, along with items of his own clothing – his 'offending gear' – in hedgerows as he walked home after breaking into someone's house.

One of the gloves that had been found discarded in bushes was made of dark-blue acrylic fibres. When we examined these fibres, we found they matched some on the surface of Peter Dixon's belt, shorts and jumper, on leg tapings taken from his body, and on exposed parts of Gwenda Dixon's body and her sweatshirt. More of the same sorts of fibres – from the pair of gloves – were also found on the broken branches with which Cooper had tried to conceal the bodies in undergrowth near the edge of a cliff, and in samples from his home. But it was a tiny flake of blood that proved to be the 'golden nugget' that helped to solve the case.

In another case of serial killings, the bodies of five young women were discovered over a period of just a few days in December 2006 at different locations in the town of Ipswich, Suffolk. All of the women had been asphyxiated – by strangulation or smothering, or both – and their naked bodies were all found outside, two of them in a brook, another in woodland, and two of them only a few yards apart near the side of a road.

DNA was found on the bodies of the last two victims, and the FSS, who were handling most of the forensic aspects of the case, reported that this matched the profile on the National DNA Database of a local fork-lift-truck driver called Steven Wright. Wright's DNA had been loaded on to the database five years earlier in connection with a theft from a hotel in Felixstowe, where he was working as a barman at the time. As soon as the match was made, he was arrested and charged with the murders of all five women.

The fact that two of the bodies were found in water made certain aspects of the forensic investigation more complicated than they might otherwise have been. And it was in connection with toxicology and, in particular, any drug that might have been administered to the women around the times of their deaths, that our help was sought. At Wright's trial in 2008, it was the DNA evidence and some textile-fibre links, as well as CCTV evidence involving the dark-blue Ford Mondeo he drove, that helped to convict the man the media dubbed 'the Suffolk Strangler'. Steven Wright was sentenced to life in prison for the murders of Tania Nicol, Gemma Adams, Anneli Alderton, Paula Clennell and Annette Nicholls – with the recommendation that he should spend the rest of his life behind bars.

Sometimes, the problem with the investigation of serial killings is that perpetrators change their *modus operandi*. For example, the Yorkshire Ripper started off with stones in a sock to incapacitate his victims and quickly progressed to using a hammer, before also stabbing them with a sharp-bladed implement. Also, while the majority of his crimes were committed in Yorkshire, a few were carried out on the other side of the Pennines. Other serial offenders – such as Robert Napper – start with rapes before moving on to murdering their victims.

So it can be difficult to know whether the cases are actually linked – such as the deaths in Wales of Florence Evans in 1989 and of Megan and Harry Tooze in 1993, which some people believe may also have involved convicted serial killer John Cooper. In some instances – such as the five 'silver surfer' cases that occurred in Cheshire between 1996 and 2011 – it may also be difficult to know whether two related deaths are double murders or murder/suicides, and/or whether some of those that are double murders have been committed by the same person. The 'silver surfer' cases were assumed to be murder/suicides, but some people now believe they may actually have been double murders perpetrated by a serial killer.

When investigating serial offences, you have to include previous cases that are thought to be part of the same series and have gone cold. And that requires pulling out all the stops because, by their very nature, cold cases are those that weren't easily solved at the time. Serial offences also place an extra burden on both investigators and the forensic scientists who are assisting them. This is because everyone in the team knows only too well that, as the days pass, there is every possibility that there will be another victim; and when the lab phone rings, you always fear the worst.

24

Textile fibres

What forensic scientists are referring to when they talk about textile fibres are not, as one might imagine, threads shed by items of clothing that are large enough to be visible easily to the naked eye – like threads from a reel of sewing cotton, for example. The sort of textile fibres that usually prove so useful as evidence are actually microscopic fragments – often less than 1 mm long – of individual filaments of natural or synthetic material that, when twisted together, make up those threads. When examined, compared under a microscope and analysed, these fibres can provide a wealth of information.

One case in which textile fibres formed an integral part of the forensic evidence that helped to convict a killer involved the murder of eight-year-old Sarah Payne.

Sarah was abducted on the evening of 1 July 2000, while playing with her siblings near her grandparents' house in West Sussex. When her body was found sixteen days later, partially buried at the edge of a field, the nationwide search became a murder investigation. Within hours, registered sex offender Roy Whiting was being interviewed by Sussex Police – for a second time since Sarah's disappearance. But with insufficient evidence to implicate him in her abduction and murder, Whiting was released from custody after two days of questioning.

Roy Whiting lived about five miles (8 km) away from where Sarah had gone missing. When he was first questioned by police, within twenty-four hours of her abduction, a petrol receipt issued by a garage on the A24 that was found in his van cast doubt on his alibi for the relevant evening. Then, three days after Sarah's body was discovered, a shoe that was identified as hers by her mother was found at the side of the road in a village just three miles (5 km) away from the same garage. Three days later, Whiting was arrested when he crashed a stolen car at high speed while being chased by the police.

While Whiting was serving a 22-month prison sentence for car theft and dangerous driving, forensic tests were carried out on his van as part of the ongoing police investigation. A forensic soil expert who examined mud that was found on a spade in Whiting's shed and inside the wheel arch of the van stated that it matched the soil at the deposition site of Sarah's body. What also caught the attention of the police was the fact that Whiting had recently had the inside of the rear of his van re-lined.

Forensic scientists working in entomology, soils, archaeology and palynology were to become involved in the case. (Entomology is the study of insects; palynology is the study of pollen grains.) But in the end, a significant part of the forensic evidence turned out to be fibre related.

The original forensic investigation for the prosecution, which was carried out at the Metropolitan Police Forensic Science Laboratory in London, was led by forensic biologist Ray Chapman. Among the forensic evidence Ray found to connect Whiting to the crime was a single hair that could have come from Sarah on a red sweatshirt that belonged to the suspect and was found in his van.

Red polyester fibres from Whiting's sweatshirt were also found in combings from Sarah's hair and on her shoe. A single printed cotton fibre with three colours along its length, which was caught in the Velcro fastening of one of her shoes, could have come from a printed cotton curtain in the back of Whiting's van. Dark-blue polyester fibres from the seat cover and multi-coloured cotton fibres from the curtain were found on the body. And some very rare, pigmented polyester fibres from Sarah's socks were discovered in the van (as well as on the body bag and her shoe).

The hair on the suspect's sweatshirt was more or less discounted as evidence after a defence expert showed that the outside of the exhibit bag containing Sarah's hairbrush was contaminated with her hair, which could also, theoretically, have contaminated other exhibits. But this still left the textile-fibre evidence; it was now more important than ever that this should be as robust as possible. It was against this background, and with only three weeks to go before Whiting was due to stand trial for murder, that the police asked hair and fibre expert Roger Robson to check the evidence and see if he agreed with Ray, and if any further fibre links could be identified.

When Roger looked at the fibres, he found that while the red dyestuff in those from the red sweatshirt was relatively pure and produced a sharp peak on the microspectrophotometry (MSP) graph, there was an additional small hump on the graph indicating an extra colour component. To check whether this extra hump was unusual, or if fibres from all sweatshirts of the same type produced the same result, he then looked at ten more examples of the same garment. While all of them had the sharp peak on the MSP graph, none of them had the extra hump. This actually made the prosecution's evidence stronger, because it showed that the hump was unusual and must have been associated with the particular batch of dye used for Whiting's sweatshirt.

While looking for any other fibres that might link the suspect with the victim, Roger examined a pair of Whiting's socks that had been found in his van. The socks were made of what is known as 'shoddy' material, comprising shredded waste fabric that includes a wide assortment of fibres. Among the fibres were some misshapen strands of colourless polyester that appeared not to have been formed properly during the manufacturing process, but had probably been used to bulk up the material. When two of the same fibres were found on the Velcro fastening of one of Sarah's shoes, the support provided by the fibre evidence linking Whiting and Sarah began to look even more interesting.

In February 2001, while still serving a sentence for the motoring offences, Roy Whiting was charged with the abduction and murder of Sarah Payne. At his trial at Lewes Crown Court later that year, he was convicted on both charges and sentenced to life in prison. In a subsequent ruling in 2010, the minimum sentence of fifty years that had been set by the Home Secretary in 2002 was reduced to forty years by the Court of Appeal.

Following a campaign by Sarah Payne's parents, the Child Sex Offender Disclosure Scheme was introduced in England and Wales in 2008. Known as Sarah's Law, it enables parents, carers and guardians to ask the police if someone who has contact with their own child or a child close to them has a record for child sex offences.

The transfer of fibres from other textiles as well as clothing – such as bedding, soft furnishings and car seats – can provide evidence of an association between one or more particular individuals and a crime scene. For example, fibres found on the body or clothing of a murder victim might match those of a suspect's clothing – as in the case described above – or other fibres discovered on the seat of their car. Or a burglar who breaks a window to gain access to a property might snag their clothing and leave behind fibre fragments on the broken glass as they climb in.

The examination of tapings and comparison of the textile fibres that have adhered to them involve three main phases: microscopy, MSP and Fourier-transform infra-red spectroscopy (FTIR). Microscopy allows magnified images of fibres from two different sources to be compared side by side, while MSP specifically analyses the colour of the fibres. And when used for man-made fibres, FTIR can indicate what they're made of and distinguish between nylon, polyester and acrylic, for example, and some sub-types of them. Also, although largely made redundant by the increasing discrimination of MSP, a fourth type of analysis is still occasionally conducted. This is thin-layer chromatography (TLC), which enables the often-complex mixture of dye components in one fibre to be separated out and compared directly with those of other fibres.

There are various factors that affect the suitability of an item of clothing as a potential source of transferred fibres. One of them is how readily it sheds its fibres: the more easily they break off, the more of them there will be on the surface of the item that are then available for transfer to other items. Another factor is how deeply dyed the individual fibres are: the more striking the colour, the easier it is to pick out the fibres among the many others that may adhere to the tapings.

Also relevant is how commonly occurring the fibres are in the textile-fibre population as a whole. It would not be worth looking for fibres from commonly available and popular items such as blue denim jeans, for example, as the evidence they would provide of an association with a specific potential source will be very weak. Depending on the circumstances, the scientist may try to discover who manufactured the fabric from which a critical item was made, how many items were manufactured, and how and where these were distributed for sale.

What also needs to be borne in mind when interpreting any kind of textile-fibre evidence is how many fibres have been transferred, and of how many different types, and whether they were transferred in both directions or in one direction only. Other points to consider are whether there were any potential legitimate sources from which the fibres could alternatively have come, and how they might have ended up where they were found – including whether the evidence could be explained by some sort of contamination.

An article that was published in August 2020 in the journal *Forensic Science International* describes a study conducted by researchers at the University of Nottingham into the potential for the airborne transfer of fibres in small, confined spaces. During the study, the fibres of the upper-body clothing worn by two people were tagged fluorescently. The two individuals then stood in the opposite corners of a lift as it operated normally, with people entering and leaving it. When the items of clothing were subsequently photographed using ultraviolet imagery, relatively high numbers of textile fibres were discovered to have been transferred between them.

The significance of this study – and of many similar studies – to forensic investigations is that it confirmed that textile-fibre fragments can be transferred in all sorts of situations and do not necessarily require direct contact between the items concerned. This is something that has actually been known about for many years, including, for example, in connection with how far loose airborne fibres can travel in a laboratory while clothing is being examined. It is one of the reasons why anti-contamination processes and procedures are so important in forensic laboratories.

All of the information described above will enable the scientist to assess the likely significance of specific textile-fibre evidence to both the prosecution and defence assertions about what happened in a particular case. In general terms, this will range from assessments that it provides no evidence to support the specific assertion, through limited evidence, moderate evidence, strong evidence, very strong evidence, extremely strong evidence, to conclusive evidence.

During the years when almost all forensic science in England and Wales was carried out in the government-run laboratories of the FSS, and there were funds available for general databasing, the results of fibre analysis on (I think) every sixth case were logged on a central computer. This enabled scientists who found matching fibres while examining a case to interrogate the database in order to establish how many times the same sort of fibre type had previously been encountered. Obviously, these data were skewed, as they came from a specific population of people whose clothing had been examined in forensic science laboratories. So they may not have been a representative sample of the population as a whole. But they did give a very general idea of roughly how often a particular fibre type might occur in garments and other items.

The traces captured on tapings are tiny, and are examined in the laboratory under a low-power microscope. If any fibres, hairs or other particles of potential interest are located, these are removed and mounted individually on glass microscope slides. Examining tapings is therefore a laborious, time-consuming – and thus potentially expensive – process, which doesn't sound very 'high-tech' in comparison to all the science and technology involved in obtaining a DNA profile, for example. But it is the very important starting point for a lot of investigations and, in the right hands, can yield an extraordinary amount of evidence.

One example of fibres on tapings turning out to be an important part of the forensic evidence was in the investigation into the murder of 79-year-old Joan Albert.

When Joan Albert's body was found in the hallway of her home in Suffolk in December 2001, she had been stabbed five times with a knife from her own kitchen. It looked to the police like a burglary gone wrong, and it wasn't long before one of her neighbours – a petty criminal called Simon Hall – became a suspect.

Hall was not a match for DNA and fingerprints found at the scene of the crime. But tapings taken from the body revealed a large number of short, black, polyester fibres of uniform length that are known as flock fibres. During the manufacture of flock fabric, these fibres are caused to stand up on end, closely packed together, to create a velvet-like finish. When they break away from their backing, they form short, uniform lengths. Although no source for the fibres was found in the suspect's home, they were abundant on tapings taken by police from the surfaces of items inside his wardrobe.

At his trial at Norwich Crown Court in 2003, Simon Hall was convicted of murder and sentenced to a minimum of fifteen years in prison. As it turned out, however, that wasn't the end of the case.

Hall had always maintained that he was innocent, and in 2007, after his wife became active in publicising his case as a miscarriage of justice, his conviction was the subject of an investigation by the BBC programme *Rough Justice*. When an independent forensic scientist was subsequently appointed by the Criminal Cases Review Commission (CCRC), he checked the original fibre evidence that had been provided for the prosecution by a scientist at the FSS. What he concluded was that the MSP results showed that the fibres found on the victim did not match those on the tapings from Hall's wardrobe.

When the case was later reviewed for appeal at the High Court in London, Suffolk Police instructed fibres expert Roger Robson to act as arbiter between the FSS and the CCRC-appointed independent forensic scientist. As well as doing more work on the fibres using MSP, Roger was able to convince the FSS to do a TLC test to check the components of the dyestuff used to colour the fibres. This showed that the fibres from Hall's wardrobe and those taken from the victim's body were actually of two overlapping (i.e. with some features in common) but subtly different types.

A link between the fibres *was* established, however, when Roger found one of each of the two types fused together on a taping from the victim's face. One possible explanation for the slight difference in the two fibre populations was that one type had fallen off the source naturally – from worn areas on the outer surface, for example – while the other might have been more deeply embedded in the fabric of the source, and only dislodged by force exerted during the struggle.

Although the independent forensic scientist did not agree with Roger's findings, the court was presumably persuaded, and Simon Hall lost his appeal. But the CCRC was still convinced that he was the victim of a miscarriage of justice. So they then contacted Roger with a view to instructing him to find out why they had lost the case and to prepare for a potential appeal to the European Court of Human Rights. Having checked that it would be possible for him to switch from working for the prosecution to the defence, it was a request Roger was happy to agree to.

One of several avenues Roger was keen to explore was a new type of chemical analysis of fibre dyes involving liquid chromatography-mass spectrometry (LC-MS). The technique had been developed in the Netherlands so, before starting on the work, Roger decided to go there to find out more about it. While he was on his way to the airport, he received a phone call informing him that, after writing a note admitting his guilt, Simon Hall had committed suicide by hanging himself in his prison cell.

In contrast to normal taping, which involves applying the same strip of sticky tape sequentially over a surface, one-to-one taping – also known as fibre mapping – involves applying strips of tape that correspond exactly to the area of the surface from which each taping is taken. The advantage of the one-to-one method of recovering fibres – and any other types of traces of interest – is that it allows their individual, precise positions to be recorded. This can provide valuable information about the extent and type of contact that resulted in their transfer.

One of the first UK cases to which the technique was applied – and which very clearly demonstrated its value – involved the death of a man whose body was found by a female visitor in the living room of his home.

The victim, who was lying on his back on the floor with his head between the legs of an upturned stool, was wearing pyjamas and a dressing gown and had a large wound in his neck. Only one of the Thames Valley Police officers who were called to the house touched the dead man before the crime scene was cordoned off and examined by a forensic pathologist. Then scenes of crime officers in hooded crime-scene suits, gloves and masks collected trace evidence, including by applying transparent adhesive strips measuring approximately six by two inches (15 x 5 cm) to the entire surface of the victim's body, comprising both his clothing and exposed skin.

After all the tapings had been numbered and their positions recorded using video, photographs and sketches, they were stuck on to individual sheets of clear plastic and sealed inside polythene bags. The same process was also applied to the floor, furniture and various other sites around the body (excluding any that were heavily bloodstained) with which the offender might have come into direct contact. Then all the tapings were taken to the forensic laboratory for examination.

A forensic scientist also examined the crime scene, paying particular attention to the distribution of blood around the body and to some bloodstains on drawers and wardrobes in the bedrooms upstairs. The wire to the telephone had been cut and the handset was missing, and some signs of disturbance in the bedrooms suggested that a rough search may have been made by the assailant.

Examination of the elderly man's body by a pathologist revealed a single wound on the left side of his neck and a small, incised, defence-type wound on his left thumb. There were also oval-shaped bruises on his arms – four on the right upper arm, one on the left – which were typical of the sort of bruises that occur when someone's arms are tightly gripped.

A few days after the body was discovered, a bin liner containing various items of clothing was found by a member of the public in woodland a few miles from the deceased man's home. Later that same day, police arrested a local man after receiving information that he had been talking about being involved in the attack.

During the five interviews the police had with the suspect, he said consistently that he had been at the deceased man's house on the day he died, but changed his story at each interview in relation to how much contact he had had with the victim. Meanwhile, the fibre evidence linking the suspect to the abandoned clothes was growing, and other evidence had also started to come to light.

DNA analysis of a spot of (possibly sprayed) blood on the left sleeve of a red hooded top that was among the items found in the bin liner provided a DNA profile that matched that of the victim. The same was true of the major contributor to a mixed profile obtained from a smear of blood from at least two individuals on the upper leg of a pair of black tracksuit bottoms. The nature and distribution of the blood on the tracksuit bottoms indicated that attacker and victim had been in close physical contact after the latter started bleeding. The fact that some of the bloodstains on the hooded top appeared to be diluted suggested that an attempt had been made to wash the blood off it. But it was the fibre examination that added another dimension to the evidence.

An integral part of any examination for evidence of transfer of textile fibres is the ability to find any that might have come from the suspect's clothing and distinguish them from those emanating from elsewhere – including the victim's clothing and furnishings at the scene itself, such as carpets, cushions and upholstery. In this instance, the outside of the abandoned tracksuit bottoms was made of black acrylic, while the inside was a mixture of many different types of fibres. The top was made of five different types of fibre, with the main fabric consisting of two types of red acrylic fibres.

What complicated matters was the fact that the red fibres from the abandoned top were of a very similar shade to the red cotton fibres of the victim's dressing gown. But, using a new fluorescence stereomicroscope, it was possible to distinguish quickly between them, on the basis that the red cotton fibres fluoresced slightly whereas the acrylics didn't. And when the number of relevant fibres on each taping from the body was counted and their distribution plotted, it was discovered that there were more than 300 red and in excess of 100 black fibres that were indistinguishable from those found on the two examined items of abandoned clothing. (There were also five red cotton fibres and one blue acrylic fibre on the abandoned top and tracksuit bottoms, which could have come from the victim's dressing gown.)

Another significant discovery was that the heaviest concentrations of red fibres were around the victim's arms, chest and right leg, with the black fibres mostly distributed around his abdomen, particularly on its upper left side. Taken together, these results indicated that, contrary to the suspect's explanation of events, there *had* been contact between the deceased man and his assailant while the victim was on the ground.

Combined with the forensic evidence and other observations from the crime scene, it seemed likely that the victim had been dragged – probably by the right leg – to the position in which he was found. His assailant had then sat astride him, gripping his right arm and shoulder and leaning forward. This would explain the pressure on the victim's upper-left abdomen and was commensurate with the fact that the knife wound that caused his death was on the left side of his neck, having been inflicted by the right hand of his attacker.

At the suspect's trial, the textile-fibre evidence combined with the blood, DNA and pathology evidence was enough to convince the jury that the suspect was guilty of murder. At the conclusion of the trial, the judge remarked that the fibre evidence was both fascinating and compelling.

Textile fibres have always been one of my favourite forms of trace evidence. This is because they are tremendously versatile, being able to demonstrate both direct and indirect links between people, places and objects, even when original source items are not available. They are capable of providing very strong evidence in their own right, but can also lead the scientist to other evidence simply by providing an indication of what are the critical items in the case on which most attention should be focused. Also, the fact that textile fibres are usually not visible to the naked eye means there is less likelihood that attempts will have been made to remove them. And even if such attempts *have* been made, these are seldom entirely successful.

Currently, however, one of the most disappointing and concerning things about investigations involving textile fibres is that they are still relatively expensive. This is because the process relies heavily on manual manipulation and microscopy, and therefore tends to take a bit of time and money.

This makes fibre examinations unpopular with the police, whose forensic budgets are under permanent stress.

There are modern imaging technologies in the scientific community that, with a bit of adjustment, are capable of speeding up the whole process. But, unfortunately, forensic research and development are so poorly funded that there seems to be little or no chance of the necessary work ever being commissioned.

Meanwhile, police forces authorise less and less work involving textile fibres, to the extent that there are now dangerously few forensic fibre experts still practising, as a result of which we will all ultimately be the losers. For example, two of the most high-profile UK cold cases in recent times were the Stephen Lawrence case and the Pembrokeshire Coastal Path and associated murders. In each of these, it was textile-fibre examinations that provided the first evidential links and that pointed the way for the all-important DNA evidence to be found, and, ultimately, for convictions to be secured.

25

Plant material

One case that included forensic evidence related to vegetation involved two men from Belfast who were arrested in February 1987 on suspicion of plotting an Irish Republican Army (IRA) campaign in England.

For a few days before they were arrested and charged with conspiring to cause explosions and possessing explosive substances and firearms with intent to endanger life, Patrick McLaughlin and Liam McCotter had been kept under surveillance by the police. During that time, they had been followed on visits to two forests in the Manchester area, where witnesses described having seen them digging and burying items.

The forensic evidence examined by three scientists at the Metropolitan Police Forensic Science Laboratory was related to soil and vegetation, plastic bags, mastic tape and grease, sacking, sheeting, dusters and nylon tights. The conclusion the scientists came to was that the flat in Manchester where the two men were staying, as well as a Ford Capri and Dodge van they were alleged to have used, were 'positively linked' with the sites in the two forests where buried explosives and firearms had been found.

When I was called in to check some of the evidence on behalf of the defence, I confirmed that a reference sample of soil and vegetation from the site of interest in Macclesfield

Forest consisted of a small amount of pale-grey soil and needles from one or more spruce trees (*Picea* species). By contrast, soil in a sample from the other site – in Delamere Forest – was dark brown, with a high content of humus and a large number of hemlock needles (*Tsuga* species), together with some pine (*Pinus* species).

I also confirmed that soil debris from various items of footwear in the defendants' flat, both vehicles and a spade found in the Ford Capri contained similar sorts of soil and conifer needles from the same three species of trees as the reference samples from the two forest locations. In fact, in the lumps of soil from some items, it was possible to see that the spruce needles were associated with the pale-grey soil, and that the hemlock and pine needles were associated with the darker brown, peaty soil. Also, some of the lumps of soil were composed of a layer of the pale-grey soil compressed with a layer of the dark-brown soil, indicating the sequential way in which the two had been deposited.

In order to find out how commonly the three types of trees occur in the Manchester area, I spoke to the two forest managers who looked after most of the forested areas in that part of the country. What they told me was that while spruce and pine are widespread, hemlock is only grown to a limited extent, mostly under taller trees to boost timber production in specific locations, as it can tolerate shade and wet. They also confirmed that Delamere Forest was essentially a pine forest, with hemlock planted in its wetter areas, while Macclesfield Forest had been planted with spruce and pine but no hemlock.

So even though the spruce needles provided only a weak link with Macclesfield Forest, the link between the hemlock needles and Delamere Forest was fairly good; while the *combination* of needle and soil evidence made the link more powerful in both cases. And in June 1988, after having been found guilty of the charges, Patrick McLaughlin was sentenced to twenty years in prison, and Liam McCotter to seventeen.

Forensic biologists examine all types of plant material – pollen, seeds, fruits, leaves, wood, bark and roots – to investigate both criminal and civil cases. There are various forms in which these can be important in a forensic examination. For example, grass stains on knees and elbows or on the back of clothing, as well as any associated soil staining, may be significant in cases of sexual assault. Sticks and branches may have been used as weapons, or employed for concealment purposes. Pollen can provide links with particular environments and indicate the time of year when a body might have been buried. And other parts of plants – such as the fruiting tops of cannabis – may feature in herbal mixtures and resins of interest in relation to drugs offences.

At the start of my career, we used to do a lot of the identification work ourselves, and had an impressive botanical reference collection to help us. What also often proved useful at that time was the fashion for turn-ups on trousers, which acted as traps for smaller vegetable traces. What has happened in more recent times, however, at least in connection with assaults, is that attention has become so focused on DNA, fingerprints and digital crime that many of us have lost our skills in relation to vegetation. So we are now more likely than previously to need to seek specialist botanical help.

As well as providing potential forensic evidence of links between people and places, plant material – from the yew tree, for example – may sometimes be used in the commission of a crime. The yew tree (Latin name *Taxus baccata*), with its dark-green needles, peeling bark and seeds encased in red berry-like fruits, is a conifer that can grow up to 66 feet (20 m) high. One of the oldest species of trees in Northern Europe, yew trees are commonly associated with churchyards, where they provide a haven for a wide variety of birds, squirrels and other wildlife. But in contrast to this bucolic image, the leaves – and almost every part – of the yew tree are the source of highly poisonous chemicals called taxine alkaloids. Again though, a contradiction exists in the fact that these chemicals can be developed into drugs for the treatment of cancer.

Although cases of suspected yew poisoning are rare, I remember one case that came into the laboratory involving some ground-up yew needles that had apparently been used to make a tea. The scientist working on the case researched the literature for any information that might help with the analysis, and then with interpreting the results. One of the things she discovered was a reference to four prison inmates in the US who had agreed to poison themselves with yew as part of a suicide pact. By the time the authorities became aware of this, three of the men were already dead. But the fourth was able to provide some invaluable information about differences in the timing and amounts of yew consumed by each of them.

In any event, for our case we first had to develop a new method for analysing the body samples with what was then the new process of liquid chromatography-mass spectrometry (LC-MS). (As news of our new method spread, other laboratories would get in touch with us when they had their own cases to deal with.) We then used the information from the American prison, along with other sources, to help us interpret our analytical results in terms of amounts and timings.

The fact that the structure of wood varies from one species of tree to another means that identifying splinters and fragments of wood can also sometimes provide a link between a crime scene and suspect. The main way of doing this is by examining and comparing the fragments under a microscope.

The key element of wood is xylem, which is the tissue

inside the bark of a tree trunk that conducts large quantities of water and mineral salts from the roots to the leaves and provides mechanical support. Each of the vertical and horizontal elements that xylem contains has its own variation in structure, which can be seen under a microscope in very thin sections that have been cut from the fragment and chemically stained. Using identification keys that list the main characteristics of all the different kinds of wood, it is possible to reduce sequentially the number of options on the list of possibilities until the specific hardwood or softwood is eventually identified.

When a sample that has been collected at a crime scene turns out to contain fragments of a number of different types of wood, this can provide good evidence of a connection. Conversely, where there is only one type and it is commonly occurring, the evidence will be much weaker, although it may be strengthened if, for example, some matching paint is associated with the wood, or there are the same kind of tool marks in it.

Some years ago, the tiny shavings of sawdust that are produced when wood is cut were used extensively as ballast in safes, mixed with Epsom salts or alum as protection against fire. Whenever a safe was blown open so that its contents could be stolen, these shavings would end up scattered over a wide area. As a result, pockets and the turn-ups of trousers were often good places to look for evidence that might link someone to a particular safe-blowing incident.

In one case we worked on, part of the forensic investigation focused on a chipboard panel that had been smashed by burglars in order to gain access to an Asda supermarket in a small town in West Yorkshire.

The scientists at the FSS laboratory in Wetherby had mounted the numerous fragments of wood found on the suspect's clothing on glass slides. After treating the slides to remove any air that might be trapped inside, they stained them and compared them under a microscope to similarly mounted fragments of the chipboard found at the scene. What they discovered was that some of the fragments on the clothing could have come from the chipboard panel in the supermarket.

Of particular interest were a fragment of hardwood, which was probably birch, and three fragments of softwood, one of which was identified as pine, another as either spruce or larch, and another as Douglas fir. The fact that the spruce/larch fragment had on its surface what appeared to be resin or glue suggested that it had come from manufactured board.

When I visited the lab at Wetherby on behalf of the defence, I examined some of the fragments myself, and agreed with the findings of the original investigation. What clouded the issue somewhat, however, was the fact that some other fragments of wood that had been found on and in the pockets of the suspect's clothing appeared to be quite different from any in the supermarket sample. There were also fragments in the supermarket sample that were different from any that had been found on the suspect's clothing.

As all the types of wood identified in the fragments found on the suspect's clothing are commonly encountered in chipboard, with none of them being particularly rare, the link they provided in this particular case was weak. However, the case serves to show the sort of complexity scientists can face when trying to work out what the results might mean.

Pollen grains are another type of plant material that can sometimes prove useful in forensic investigations. Pollen, the powdery substance that contains a plant's male genetic material, is easily transferred and so sticky that washing an object doesn't necessarily remove it. So it can be found in the mud on people's shoes, on their clothes, in their hair and nasal passages, on the tyres of their cars and a wide range of other objects.

Analysing the pollen found on a body can provide a link between it and a crime scene, or between a suspect and a victim. It can sometimes also help to locate the place where someone was actually killed before their body was moved to wherever it was found. But it isn't only in crimes against the person that pollen can provide pivotal evidence. It can also help to identify the country of origin of smuggled goods such as drugs and money.

One of the many cases that forensic palynologist Professor Patricia Wiltshire helped to solve involved the murder of sixteen-year-old Leanne Tiernan, who disappeared in November 2000 while on her way home from a shopping trip to Leeds.

When Leanne's body was eventually found, in woodland about fifteen miles (24 km) away in August 2001, it was wrapped in a duvet cover and a series of plastic bin liners, which were secured around her neck by a dog collar. Owing to the state of preservation of the body, medical opinion suggested that it had been kept frozen after death until a few weeks before it was discovered.

As soon as Leanne was identified by her fingerprints, West Yorkshire Police's missing-person investigation became an intensive murder investigation, which was led by my colleague of many years, head of CID, Detective Chief Superintendent Chris Gregg, and given the name Operation Conifer.

No suspects had been identified by September 2001, when Pat was asked to obtain palynology samples from Leanne's nasal passages and scalp, as well as from the duvet cover she was wrapped in. The hope was that any pollen that was present might give some indication of where Leanne's body had been kept before she was buried in Lindley Woods. It wasn't long, though, before the police had a possible suspect.

With little else to go on, they had decided to see if they could discover where the dog collar had come from. Starting with local pet shops, they established that it was made by a company in Nottingham that produced vast quantities of the same item, which they sold throughout the UK and all over the world. So they started contacting the 212 UK wholesalers that sold the collar. At number 114 on the list, they found one that supplied outlets in Leeds, and had sold six during the six months before Leanne disappeared to a man called John Taylor, who had provided his address when he paid by Visa.

Meanwhile, Pat was continuing her forensic investigation. In a paper published in 2006 in the journal *Forensic Science International*, she explained how she took soil and vegetation samples from the place where Leanne was last seen alive, from the woodland where her body was found, and from the garden of her home. She then compared the pollen samples with those she had retrieved from the body, and after examining the prepared microscope slides, she provided the police with an account of her first impressions.

The fact – gleaned from Leanne's mother – that Leanne washed her hair every other day was to help in the identification of another place where some of the pollen had got into her hair before, at the time of, or after her death. During the post-mortem examination, Leanne's body and hair had inevitably become contaminated by plant debris from the outside of the plastic bin liners that were wrapped around her when she was found. So it was decided to disregard from the palynological profile any pollen and spores from species of plants found in the place from which she was abducted, from Lindley Woods (where she was found), and from the garden of her home.

What remained in the profile from Leanne's hair included a large quantity of microscopic fragments of charcoal and other elements of burnt wood, together with fungal spores. This led Pat to the conclusion that it had been in contact with soil and wood ash for a significant period of time, as well as in direct contact with vegetation and/or the ground.

The palynological profiles of Leanne's body and the bed cover it was wrapped in were very similar to each other. But they were very different from the profiles from her garden, the abduction site, and the site in Lindley Woods. When the percentages of the different species present were analysed and tabulated, they produced a picture of either a weed-filled garden or waste ground near a garden, where the body would have been placed close enough to the remains of a bonfire – on which both soft and hard woods had been burned – for some elements of it to have become lodged in her hair.

The species of plants identified as growing close to where the body had lain included privet, elder, hawthorn, brambles, poplar, beech and *Prunus* (which could have been sloe, plum or cherry), as well as various herbaceous plants such as grasses and nettles.

With all this information in hand, the police officers who went to John Taylor's house immediately recognised the small back garden. Bordered by poplar trees and a neglected hedge of privet and elder, it also contained all the other species of plants that had been identified, as well as the remains of two bonfires.

Samples were then collected from the garden and compared with the pollen types and average percentages of all the samples that had been discovered on Leanne's body and the bed cover. What was found was that the profiles were consistent in terms of species of pollen and spores, fungal remains, elements of charred wood and other fragments. It was even possible to identify where in the garden Leanne had lain, with her hair in the ash of one of the bonfires.

As well as strong palynological evidence linking Leanne to Taylor's garden, there was other forensic evidence. DNA testing of the root attached to a hair that was caught in the knot of a scarf around Leanne's neck provided a DNA profile that matched Taylor's. Analysis of some twine found on Leanne's body proved an exact match for some found in Taylor's house. Some yellow cable ties on his fence and some green plastic were similarly matched, as were some red nylon carpet fibres that remained caught on nails in the floorboards of his house after he had apparently removed and burned all the carpeting.

Faced with all the forensic evidence, John Taylor admitted to murdering Leanne Tiernan. And in July 2002, he was sentenced to serve a minimum of twenty-five years in prison, which was increased four years later to thirty years.

My first degree was in botany, so I have been interested in all the different facets of it for a very long time, and I remember being delighted when I realised what an important part it could play in forensic casework. The importance of botany lies partly in the fact that there is a lot of vegetation about, to the extent that it's very difficult to do anything much outdoors without leaving signs that you've walked or sat down where you have and picked up grass stains, for example, or fragments of vegetation on your clothes.

Botany is also incredibly varied, reflecting all the different parts of a plant, and all the different species of plants that exist just in this country alone. Some of those parts – such as pollen grains and spores – are absolutely minute. Therefore criminals are very unlikely to realise that substantial amounts of them might be present on critical items in a case. Then there's the soil that might be associated with the vegetation, and that can tell a whole story of its own in terms of its general nature and precisely where it was found, as well as its detailed chemical analysis. All of which means that committing a crime outdoors is no 'safer' from the criminal's point of view than committing one inside, so far as the likelihood of evading detection is concerned.

26

Unsolved cases

Given an adequate budget, a team of the right sort of scientists, and access to the range of highly sophisticated scientific techniques available to forensic scientists today, I have come to the surprising conclusion that there are few cases that can't be solved. There will always be some people who slip through the net, for one reason or another, and some who get away with murder. But as we have proved ourselves by helping to solve many cold cases, including several high-profile ones, the evidence is usually there somewhere, and may be found if the opportunity arises to go back and look for it in the right sort of way.

Some unsolved cases stay with you for years, popping into your mind at unexpected moments. If you know enough about them, you sometimes think of new approaches that could be taken, or new technologies that could be used to try to solve them. So what is it that causes some of those cases to be particularly memorable and others less so?

I think first and foremost must be a feeling of real injustice – a wrong that needs to be righted insofar as possible. One prime example was the murder of seventeen-year-old Claire Woolterton, whose naked, mutilated body was found on a towpath in Windsor in August 1981 (see Chapter 6). The fact that no crime scene had ever been identified made solving the case even more difficult. So it was very satisfying when samples I had taken from her body all those years ago yielded the DNA that finally identified and helped to convict her killer in 2013.

In other cases, there might have been some evidence that, for whatever reason, wasn't quite enough to convince a judge and jury – as in the early years of the Stephen Lawrence case, for example. Or failings in the original investigation might be exposed which, if they could be compensated for, could theoretically still yield the critical evidence – as perhaps in the case involving the disappearance of three-year-old Madeleine McCann from a holiday apartment in Portugal in May 2007. Or the case might be reminiscent of another one, and might eventually be solved when it turns out that the same perpetrator was responsible for both – which might conceivably happen in relation to the murders in July 1993 of Megan and Harry Tooze.

In January 1995, the trial began in Newport Crown Court of a man called Jonathan Jones, who was accused of murdering the couple at their farm in the Welsh village of Llanharry. The motive for the killings was thought to be the £150,000 that would be inherited by their daughter, Cheryl, who was Jones's fiancée.

According to the prosecution, after travelling to Llanharry from the house in Orpington in Kent where he and Cheryl lived, Jonathan Jones shot Megan and Harry Tooze at close range with a shotgun. After hiding the bodies under an assortment of hay bales and other farmyard items in a cowshed on their property, he then returned home on foot and by rail. That same evening, as concern for the missing couple began to mount, Jones drove back to Llanharry in his car. Shortly before he arrived at about 3.15 a.m., police officers who were already at the farm found Harry's body. By the time Megan's body was also discovered, Jones was on his way home again, to comfort his distressed fiancée.

We became involved in the case when we were asked by Jones's solicitor to examine the prosecution's forensic evidence. It was forensic biologist Russell Stockdale who visited the FSS laboratories at Chepstow to discuss the findings and examine some of the evidential items for himself. He then went to Llanharry to familiarise himself with the crime scene, the locality and the route to the train station that the killer was thought to have taken.

The inside of the cowshed at the couple's farm was divided into pens, each of which had a stone feeding trough at one end. Harry Tooze's body had been discovered lying face down in the trough in the first pen, hidden under empty barley bags, sacking and hay bales, and with a wall of plastic crates and other junk piled up in front of it. Megan's body was lying parallel to Harry's, along what would have been the feed access corridor, and was covered with similar items, topped by a rusty milk churn, tarpaulins, plastic and carpet.

Two separate and distinct areas of bloodstaining seemed to mark the place where each of them had been killed – just inside one of the two doors into the cowshed in Harry's case, and outside, at the far corner of the front of the house, in Megan's.

Jonathan Jones was only one of at least four suspects at that time. But no traces of blood that could have come from Megan or Harry and no fibres of potential evidential significance were found in or on the items that belonged to him. These items included his car, twelve pairs of trousers, seventeen jackets and numerous other clothing, sixteen pairs of footwear, and eight bags and cases. Some of the blood found on items belonging to the other suspects could be eliminated from the investigation, and the results of tests carried out on others proved inconclusive.

What was interesting about these particular findings was the fact that, as both victims had been shot at close range, it is likely that some of their blood and/or tissue would have been expected to be on the assailant himself, his clothing and the weapon. The fact that the bodies had clearly been moved from where they were shot to where they were found meant that further substantial transfer of blood and/or body tissue would also have been expected to have occurred to the assailant's hands and clothes. Therefore, it was Russell's opinion that whoever killed the couple must have been heavily blood-stained, particularly on his lower clothing and footwear, and that his face and upper clothing could also have been speckled with their blood when the shots were fired.

The FSS scientist had examined three sink traps taken from the kitchen sink, bathroom sink and bath at the farm, and had found no significant reaction to the leucomalachite green (LMG) test for blood. This raised the issue of how and where the assailant had cleaned himself of the considerable amount of bloodstaining that would have been present on him and his clothing.

If the assailant had been Jonathan Jones, as the police suspected, he had various options. For example, he could have had a vehicle parked nearby and arrived at the farm with the shotgun concealed, perhaps in a bag, and with a complete set of clothes that he changed into before he left. Or he might have walked to the nearest railway station or to catch a bus. But both those possibilities would have involved passing through residential streets while bloodstained and with the shotgun that he had apparently taken with him when he left the farm, as the police had searched for it without success.

The first option seemed more likely than travelling on public transport in bloodstained clothing. But a meticulous and widespread search carried out by the police failed to reveal the clothes he would have changed out of, the shotgun he used to kill both of his victims, the bag in which he had presumably concealed it, or any spent cartridges. In fact, as

Russell wrote in the summary to his report, there was not one shred of forensic evidence to link Jones with the killings. Indeed, at his trial in 1995, the only 'evidence' against him was a fingerprint that had been found on a cup in the kitchen at the farm – despite which, he was found guilty and given two life sentences.

In an unusual turn of events following the trial, a letter was apparently sent to the Home Secretary by the judge who had sentenced Jonathan Jones. In it, the judge expressed concern about the verdict and said that he was surprised the jury had convicted the accused. Clearly, he wasn't the only one to have doubts, and in April 1996 the convictions were quashed when three judges at the Court of Appeal in London ruled them 'unsafe'. After his release from prison, Jonathan Jones married Cheryl Tooze, who had always believed in his innocence.

In 2003, we were called in to advise on aspects of the case. But it wasn't long before the murder investigation was scaled down, and whoever killed Megan and Harry Tooze still remains to be identified.

There are many features of this case that are reminiscent of the double murder of brother and sister Richard and Helen Thomas in their isolated farmhouse in Wales, and the associated killings of Gwenda and Peter Dixon on the Pembrokeshire Coastal Path. *So* many, in fact, that the obvious place to start a re-investigation would be with John Cooper, who was convicted of those killings. Of course, the deaths of Megan and Harry Tooze might be nothing to do with Cooper. But we know so much about him and his *modus operandi* that it shouldn't take long to find out.

Another currently unsolved case involves the death in 2010 of an MI6 spy called Gareth Williams. When Williams was discovered inside a padlocked holdall in the bath in his flat, a murder investigation was launched. The keys to the padlock were also inside the bag, and there was a single hair on the dead man's hand, which forensic scientists said belonged to someone other than Williams. It wasn't possible to extract a DNA profile from the hair, perhaps because it was too short or had no root attached to it. But the DNA of two unidentified people was found on the holdall and on a towel in the flat – one of whom was subsequently eliminated from the investigation when he was identified as a member of lab staff, whose DNA had become involved as a result of inadvertent contamination (see Chapter 21).

The conclusion of an inquest held in 2012 was that Williams had probably been unlawfully killed by a person or persons unknown. The following year, the police announced that the likely cause of death was an accident after Williams had shut himself in the holdall. So the case remains unsolved. But bearing in mind the traces that have already been discovered, and the advances in both forensic techniques and scientific investigative approaches that have occurred since then, a scientific review would certainly be worthwhile.

Another unsolved case – which has stayed with me ever since I first heard about it – involved the death in the early hours of 31 March 2001 of 31-year-old Stuart Lubbock.

Stuart had been attending a party at the Essex home of entertainer Michael Barrymore when his body was found in the swimming pool. None of the other guests seemed to be able to shed any light on what had happened. And, initially, Stuart's death was assumed to have been a tragic accident – which may explain why the scene was not immediately secured and subjected to a detailed examination of the sort that might have helped to determine what had taken place. This became all the more regrettable when it was discovered during the post-mortem examination of Stuart's body that he had suffered severe anal injuries indicative of a serious sexual assault shortly before he died. Also, the cause of death was complicated by extensive attempts at resuscitation, to the extent that it was not possible to say whether he had died as a result of drowning or from some other cause.

Since then, a large amount of forensic work has been conducted on items from the scene and from some of the people who were there that night – all, as yet, to no avail. But it is certainly far too early to give up on the case, not least for the sake of Stuart's family, who deserve to have answers to their questions.

There are many reasons why it's important to continue to try to resolve unsolved cases. These include providing closure for victims' families and some sense that justice has been done for the precious lives that have been taken from them. Another reason is to ensure that dangerous people are taken off the streets for safer, more secure communities. And another is to improve public confidence in law enforcement so that we are happy to pay for it and comply with the rule of law.

All this was brought into sharp focus by a recent meeting I had with one of the original five defendants charged with the murder of Lynette White in Cardiff in 1988, three of whom ended up being convicted. Two years later, the convictions of the men – who became known as the Cardiff Three as they protested their innocence – were overturned when it became evident that the confession made by one of them had been forced out of him by extreme bullying tactics employed by the police at the time. There had been absolutely no forensic evidence to link the three men with the crime.

The problem was that until our re-investigation revealed DNA that indicated it was a night watchman by the name of Jeffrey Charles Gafoor who was actually to blame for Lynette's death, many people continued to believe that the original defendants were guilty and had got off on a technicality.

It was the extended period of life-destroying unfairness that the defendant in the Lynette White case I spoke to was able to describe so patiently and so eloquently, and I shall never forget it. Just as I will never forget the quiet determination and dignity of Terry Lubbock, who spent years fighting to understand what happened to his son Stuart on the night he was found in Michael Barrymore's swimming pool with horrific injuries that have never been explained, and shortly after which he died. Sadly, Terry Lubbock died in September 2021, but other members of the family and their friends are continuing the fight for justice for him.

The idea that forensic science can improve fairness and faith in our criminal justice system is one of the things that first attracted me to it as a career. Discovering how true that is – not just for the Cardiff Three, but also in many other cases over the years – has been extremely rewarding. And with all the advances in technology, matched with improved understanding of how best to deploy it, we now have the capability to solve the vast majority of unsolved cases.

27

Worrying verdicts

Sometimes, criminals remain at liberty because their crimes have not – yet – been solved. Sometimes innocent people are imprisoned because they have been wrongly convicted. And sometimes the lives of innocent people are marred by unfounded suspicion.

Every now and then, I have come across a case in which the scientific evidence just doesn't seem to stack up properly. It may be because there isn't any evidence when some would almost certainly be expected. Or it may be that the evidence is very weak, or doesn't form the right sort of pattern in the context of the case. Of course, I am only looking at the forensic aspects of the case, and there may be strong evidence elsewhere. But it is interesting how often, in these circumstances, convictions are ultimately overturned – sometimes many years later.

One example of a case involving someone who was wrongly suspected and charged, but not ultimately convicted, was the murder of Rachel Nickell. There had certainly been no forensic evidence against the suspect, and there can't have been any other type of evidence either, because after I had given a talk at a book festival recently, I was approached by someone in the audience who was part of the legal defence team that had represented him. One of the things she told me during our ensuing conversation was that she and other eminent members of the team had all been entirely convinced that long-term suspect Colin Stagg was innocent, and they were extremely concerned by the attempt to prosecute him.

It was a solicitor's concerns about his client's conviction that resulted in him returning repeatedly to another case over a period of several years.

On the morning of 9 December 1986, the naked body of 24-year-old Linda Cook was found on a patch of waste ground in Portsmouth, partially concealed by what was mostly grassy vegetation. She had been subjected to a sexual assault, her face, neck and stomach had been stamped on, and she had been strangled. A few weeks later, eighteen-year-old naval rating Michael Shirley was arrested and charged with her murder.

When Linda's body was found, her clothes and a carrier bag containing some videos she had been carrying were scattered around her, which suggested that it was where the attack had occurred. But eye-witness accounts cast doubt on whether Shirley *could* have been at the scene during the time frame in which Linda must have arrived there.

At Shirley's trial, the prosecution presented evidence from four forensic scientists. The scientist who visited the crime scene and took tapings from the body noted, among other things, its position, the distribution of the clothing both on it and beside it, and partial muddy footwear impressions on the stomach.

DNA profiling was in its infancy at that time and failed to provide any results. However, blood-grouping tests that were carried out on the mixture of semen and bloodstaining on swabs taken from the victim's vagina showed that the semen could have come from Shirley – or, indeed, from approximately 23.3 per cent of the rest of the adult male UK population. In fact, three of the fifteen other possible suspects whose blood samples were examined could have been an alternative source of the semen on the intimate swabs.

Examination of the shoes Shirley thought he had been wearing on the relevant night indicated that his right shoe could have made the muddy marks found on the victim's stomach. But there was no evidence of the transfer of any textile fibres between his clothing and Linda's.

Despite the lack of any strong forensic evidence, Michael Shirley was found guilty at his trial at Winchester Crown Court in January 1988 by a majority of eleven to one, and was sentenced to life in prison. Fifteen months later, his application to appeal against his conviction was turned down.

I first became involved in the case in 1991, when I was asked by Shirley's solicitor to review the original scientific evidence. The cause of his concern was that his client's conviction had been based purely on the fact that he *could* have killed Linda Cook, rather than on any proof to indicate that he *had* done so.

After re-examining the original evidential items, I wrote a report in which I commented on numerous facts that failed to identify Shirley as the killer. For example, the semen on the intimate swabs taken from Linda's body did not point positively to Shirley. It hadn't been possible to establish the exact size of the shoe that had made the footwear marks on the body, but they could have been made by any of the several thousand shoes with the same sole pattern and 'flash' logo that had been sold in sizes 8, 9 and 10. There was no evidence of transfer of textile fibres between Shirley's and Linda's clothes and bodies. There was no blood on any of Shirley's clothing that could have come from Linda. And statements from various eyewitnesses suggested that Shirley had been too far behind Linda in time for him to have accosted her.

Basically, I concluded that there wasn't any substantive scientific evidence to suggest that Michael Shirley had killed Linda Cook. Also, when the case went to trial, the defence may not have been aware of the potential significance of the absence of certain aspects of evidence. In the event, however, the appeal judges decided that although the conviction could not stand if it was only supported by one or two pieces of circumstantial evidence, the fact that there were four or five provided grounds to turn down the appeal.

After being contacted again by Shirley's solicitor two years later, in April 1993, I reviewed the case once more and commented on any further work that it might be possible to carry out. Then, in June 1995, he got in touch again, and asked me to apply 'the most recent newest DNA techniques' to some of the remaining material that had been taken for scientific investigation at the time of the trial.

Unfortunately, all the swabs had been destroyed by that time, as had Linda Cook's clothing, including some that was stained with semen. The only semen-contaminated samples that remained were some microscope slides made from the swabs. Although they were badly faded, to the extent that the sperm heads originally recorded were no longer visible, they at least contained enough sperm to attempt analysis using the latest DNA technique of short tandem repeat (STR) profiling. This was carried out by the FSS, but unfortunately it wasn't successful.

By that time, it wasn't only Shirley's solicitor who had doubts about his conviction: the makers of the television programme *Trial and Error* had also become involved. In February 2000, the FSS made another attempt to obtain a result – by re-testing the extract that had been prepared from the microscope slides in 1995 – and this time they identified some DNA components in it. But they were unable to interpret these, because although they had a sample from Shirley and so could work out which components could have come from him, they had no idea what Linda Cook's DNA profile might have been, as none of the evidential items from the original investigation had been retained.

Then, in 2001, a scientist at the FSS located a slide prepared from a bloodstained mouth swab taken from Linda Cook that was uncontaminated by semen and therefore suitable as a reference sample of her DNA. From the result obtained from the microscope slides made from Linda's vulval and low vaginal swabs, they subtracted the DNA components that could have come from her. And it was then possible to see that the components that were left could *not* have come from Michael Shirley.

In the comprehensive report we compiled in May 2002, we agreed with the FSS scientist that, on the assumption that the DNA from Linda's vulval and low vaginal swabs represented a mixture from Linda Cook herself and her killer, that killer could not have been Michael Shirley. But it wasn't until 2003 – after he had spent sixteen years in prison and gone on a number of hunger strikes to protest his innocence – that his conviction was quashed and he was finally cleared by the Court of Appeal. Whoever *did* kill Linda Cook has not yet been identified.

Another example of a worrying conviction concerned the murder in November 1981 of sixteen-year-old Pamela Hastie, who was raped and then strangled with some sisal twine in woodland near her home in Scotland. Raymond Gilmour, who was nineteen at the time, was known to frequent the woods and had a previous conviction for indecent exposure. So it wasn't surprising that he came to the attention of the police. But although Gilmour confessed to the crime, some aspects of his account of what had happened were clearly wrong, and he was released without charge. Then a new police superintendent took over the case, and despite the fact that Gilmour had withdrawn his confession, he was charged and ultimately convicted of Pamela's rape and murder.

After Gilmour's conviction in 1982, his solicitor continued to work on the case. In 1994, he asked if I would check the scientific evidence and compare what was found with what might have been expected if Raymond Gilmour had, indeed, been Pamela's killer.

As well as highlighting several inaccuracies in Gilmour's original confession, my investigation focused on a number of types of evidence that might have been expected to be found. These included blood, textile fibres, soil and vegetation on Gilmour himself, and paint (from his clothes) on Pamela. There were also aspects of the crime scene that had never been properly explored, such as the tapings from Pamela's body, a footwear mark, and a purple nylon fibre and three hairs on the branch of a tree. As a result of these various features, I came to the firm conclusion that the holes in the scientific evidence raised serious doubts about the safety of Gilmour's conviction.

Forensic psychologist Professor Gisli Gudjonsson had also expressed concern about Gilmour's confession, and the fact that, due to his emotional vulnerability, he would not have coped well with any pressure that might have been exerted on him by the police. But it wasn't until 2002 that Raymond Gilmour was released from prison pending an appeal, and it was to be another five years before his conviction was finally quashed.

Patterns of one kind or another are incredibly important in forensic science. They can tell you if a crime is likely to be part of a series carried out by the same criminal. They can illuminate some aspect of the sequence of events at a crime scene. And they can also indicate that something might be amiss and that the evidence could be the result of contamination or even, conceivably, deliberate planting. Sometimes, they can also highlight gaps in apparently strong evidence and indicate that the explanation for it may not be as simple as previously thought.

It was the possibly mistaken reliance on apparently strong evidence that revolved around fibres that could have come from a pair of gloves that is the source of my concerns about another case involving a murder.

Ivy Batten was eighty-four years old when she died in her home in Devon in November 1987 after being struck several times on the head with a hammer. There were some woollen fibres on the broken glass of the window that had apparently been smashed to gain access to Ivy's house, and these were found to match a pair of woollen gloves that were discovered, together with a bloodstained hammer, in a field nearby. When similar fibres were also found inside one of the pockets of a coat worn by the suspect, Brian Parsons, and in the glove compartment – but nowhere else – in his car, he was convicted of the murder and sentenced to life in prison.

A decade later, we became involved in the case when Parsons appealed against his conviction. And although his appeal was turned down, I have always had doubts about the pattern of the evidence linking him with the gloves, based on the strangely very limited and very specific areas in which the matching fibres were found. Apparently, my concerns are shared by the police who conducted an independent review of the original investigation, and by one of the lawyers – who subsequently became a judge – who was involved in the case. It seems unlikely that we are all wrong.

Another example of a death that might warrant further investigation is that of 73-year-old widow Florence Evans (see Chapter 18). In 1989, Florence's body was found, fully clothed, in a bath of cold water at her home in Pembrokeshire. A post-mortem examination revealed a cut on her head that might have caused her to lose consciousness, and a coroner found the cause of her death to be accidental. But Florence's family have always had concerns about this conclusion. And there certainly seem to be some unanswered questions that might warrant further investigation.

One possible interpretation of the events that led to Florence's death might be that she had been running a bath when she fell, banged her head and toppled into it. However, the fire in the kitchen that provided hot water hadn't been lit, so the water she had been running into the bath would have been cold. And, according to her family, she didn't take baths anyway. Also, her purse was missing, and she had apparently told friends a few days before her death that she had mislaid her house keys.

Florence Evans died shortly after the bodies of Peter and Gwenda Dixon were found nearby on the Pembrokeshire Coastal Path. And what may add to the potentially suspicious aspects of Florence's death – as acknowledged recently by the Senior Investigating Officer of 'the Pembrokeshire murders' – is the fact that serial killer John Cooper sometimes did odd jobs for her.

There are a number of reasons why forensic scientists, like me, might find certain convictions worrying. For example, if there's no forensic evidence when you'd expect it; when there *is* forensic evidence but it doesn't form the right sort of pattern; or when there's forensic evidence that, if anything, points to someone else, but just not sufficiently strongly to draw a firm conclusion. Of course, there may be good reasons why any of those might be the case. But if there aren't, it may indicate that there's something to worry about.

All forensic scientists have cases that continue to surface in their minds from time to time, and continue to trouble them when they do. Sometimes those cases are resolved; but sometimes they never are.

What's next?

Forensic science turned out to be a true vocation. It was never just a job to provide a living. And looking back over what I've written in these pages, I'm struck by the passion with which not just I, but most forensic scientists approach their work.

For instance, Denise didn't have to go to Kew Gardens to discover that the poisoner in her case had used Indian aconite. She could have just said she didn't know because she hadn't come across it before. Alex didn't have to test the puparia for heroin as a potential link to the missing body of Chantel Taylor. Nobody was expecting him to do it, as it had never been attempted before. And April didn't have to extend her search for evidence in the Stephen Lawrence case to the original packaging of the suspects' clothing. But this gave us the first full DNA profile of his blood and helped enrich our understanding of the trail of blood he had left at the crime scene. But they did. And lots of other people did lots of other things, only a mere fraction of which has been captured here. What those people have in common is a flair and determination to get to the bottom of things so that, ultimately, they can help the police to catch the real criminals and the courts to reach the right verdicts.

I hope I've managed to convey some sense of that here, to inspire new generations of forensic scientists to embrace this strange but important little corner of scientific endeavour. I hope also that I've been able to show what a vital role forensic science plays in ensuring fairness and justice in our society and therefore why it needs nurturing. In order for that to happen, however, there are some big questions that need to be asked. For example, how can we best protect and build on the knowledge and skills we have spent the last hundred years developing? How can we make the most of emerging technologies and translate these effectively for use in everyday forensic casework? And who should we entrust to deliver our impartial independent forensic services? Can this really be done by the police themselves when the main focus of their job is to hunt down and prosecute people?

Finding answers to those questions will be up to you!

Index